A Guidebook for Creating
Three-Dimensional Theatre Art

A Guidebook for Creating Three-Dimensional Theatre Art

Ann J. Carnaby

HEINEMANN
Portsmouth, NH

Heinemann
A division of Reed Elsevier Inc.
361 Hanover Street
Portsmouth, NH 03801–3912

Offices and agents throughout the world

Art credits can be found on p. 186.

Library of Congress Cataloging-in-Publication Data
Carnaby, Ann J.
    A guidebook for creating three-dimensional theatre art /
Ann J. Carnaby.
        p. cm.
    Includes bibliographical references and index.
    ISBN 0–435–07000–2
    1. Theater—Stage-setting and scenery. 2. Stage props—
Design and construction.   3. Costume.
    I. Title.
PN2091.S8C29   1997
792'.025–dc20   96-43402
                        CIP

Editor: Lisa A. Barnett
Production: Vicki Kasabian
Book and cover design: Jenny Jensen Greenleaf
Manufacturing: Louise Richardson

Printed in the United States of America on acid-free paper
01 00 99 98 97   EB   1 2 3 4 5

In the without-whom-I-would-not-have done-this category,
kudos to Barbara, Grace, and Lee:

Applause.

CONTENTS

In 1981 I first heard Fred Nihda, master props maker and creator of the Fruit of the Loom people and the horse heads and hooves for *Equus*, state that he was *not* a designer, and that he was proud to say he was a craftsperson. He went on to suggest that there was nothing wrong with being the doer and not the designer; that the doer carried, after all, the responsibility for bringing the object from concept to reality. He went on to demonstrate the "magic" of his craft. There was no doubt in my mind, from that moment on, that being the craftsperson was every bit as important, and just as rewarding as being the designer. Not long after that experience, I heard the same sentiment from Bob Moody, scenic painter for world-renowned theatrical scene designers. To all of you who may not be fortunate enough to see and hear either of these great craftspeople speak about and demonstrate their art, I will try to convey their conviction and their passion for advancing the craft of theatre art. The creation of garments, hats, props, all the pieces that help decorate a production and give it its style, its history, its purpose and intent, is a most worthy craft. The craftsperson must never see him- or herself as a second-class citizen to the designer. If anything, the two are symbiotic disciplines, each dependent on the skills of the other for the creation of the ultimate product.

I extend sincere thanks and appreciation to Fred Nihda and Bob Moody and all the role models of the theatrical craft world who have shared selflessly with us their skills, their ethic, and their secrets, that this art may live for the next generation.

Thanks to my staff who put up with endless suggestions to "try it this way" and "here's some new stuff—let's try that here." They are now much more tolerant of the notion that just because we did something a certain way last time doesn't mean we won't change it next time. I am grateful for their patience, flexibility, and spirit of adventure as we learn and grow together.

Special appreciation to Ben, who, in his role as principal lapcat and general factotum, has been with me (usually wedged between my lap and my laptop) throughout the development of this book.

The further one gets away from cities where there are centers of art, theatre, culture, and specialists in the creation of anything and everything, the more one is called upon to produce a variety of strange and wonderful objects for theatre, television, film, and promotional activities. During the past fifteen years I have been asked to supply a myriad of unique and sometimes peculiar items, all of which fall into a category I call theatre art. Most of the time these items had to be fabricated from scratch; some were modifications of existing items. Each had specific definitions of what it could and couldn't do, how it had to look, and the specific purpose it had to serve. Responding to these requests has helped me develop a certain philosophy and methodology when approaching a new project, which I present in this volume.

Fine art is defined as: "Art produced or intended chiefly for beauty rather than utility . . . something requiring highly developed techniques and skills."

Pieces of theatre art are much more restricted in their purpose, even though they may have to be just as artful in terms of how skillfully the piece is executed and how "artistic" the final result apears to be. When a craftsperson is asked to produce an object of theatre art—a tiger rug, a donkey head, the murder weapon, "fat" makeup, a ghost costume—that object may have many requirements and restrictions for its purpose and function. For example, a tiger rug may need to be engineered so it can be puppeteered to speak, its ears rigged so they can be wiggled on cue, and the entire piece light and indestructible enough to survive being whisked off the set by its tail every performance. A donkey head for A *Midsummer Night's Dream* may need to be open enough for the audience to hear the actor and to see his head and face.

The goals of this guidebook are fourfold:

1. To present a "diagnostic" approach to the decision-making process of creating a piece of theatre art
2. To break down the old barriers of specific skill

categories so that a member of a certain discipline feels free to utilize techniques and materials from other disciplines

3. To introduce new materials, tools, and techniques, *and*

4. To suggest different ways of using familiar materials, tools, and techniques.

The intent of this book is to help you become more proficient in both analytical (thinking) and crafting (doing) skills. It is also important for you to acknowledge what you are not able to do especially well. It is better to involve someone else who is more proficient than you at something—whether it's painting eyes, or drawing on flat paper, or welding steel. The finished project must not be compromised by your ego. When creating pieces of theatre art, the task is to serve the production with the best piece possible, whether you do it on your own or have some well-placed help along the way.

How This Book Is Organized

I have called this volume a guidebook and intend it to be used as a tool to guide the reader's thinking toward new and creative ways of meeting the never-ending challenges presented by live theatre or other live performance situations.

My problem-solving approach is best outlined as follows:

Identify:
appearance goals
function goals

Ensure a safe environment

Select:
tools
materials

Apply:
structure techniques
detail techniques
surface techniques

This approach represents both a philosophical and practical way to create a special item for performance. It works for any type of object—a prop, a hat, shoes, wig, makeup, a three-dimensional piece of scenery, a puppet, or a costume. It sounds simple. It is only complex because it is analytical in a way that is foreign to many of us. When one begins a project one must first find out all the details of what the piece needs to do, what it doesn't do, what it has to look like, and how it must move, fit, articulate, or otherwise perform. That is how the goal is identified. Based on the parameters identified in that first step, one can then figure out how the inside of the object needs to be built so that it meets the goal, and one can select the right tools, materials, and techniques. Decorating the surface is the final step in achieving the goal.

The information in this book builds on itself. First, how to develop a goal and a plan—the problem-solving approach. Next, how to create a safe work environment. Then selecting tools—beginning with the essentials: brain, eyes, hands—which are divided into categories by functional type. Materials are also categorized by function for ease in making the right selection. Techniques of assembling the structure, adding details, and decorating surfaces show ways to use tools and materials in varying combinations, thus putting the information from the two previous chapters together in different configurations for different purposes. A selection of projects are then presented as examples of solutions to very specific problems. Each project utilizes one or more techniques, each technique uses tools and materials in different ways depending on the specific goals of each project.

Each chapter addresses one of the steps in this process. Chapter 1 describes the process of how to approach a project of theatre art in a logical and systematic way in order to create a piece for a specific purpose in a particular production. This approach views the project piece as a problem to be solved. It starts at the goal, defining the nature of the finished piece—its form, its function, its limitations, and its appearance—then identifies the tools, materials, and techniques required to reach that goal.

Chapter 2 discusses safety in the workplace as a mandate. It is the first and most essential consideration to any project. Use the safest tools and materials available. Know the risks associated with each and how to minimize them. Know oneself and one's limitations. Obtain current information about the tools and materials being used, evaluate their risks, and seek safer alternatives. Keep your environment safe.

Chapters 3 describes the basic types of tools that are necessary and useful to the craftsperson. They are grouped according to function.

Chapter 4 surveys an array of materials, again grouped by the function each serves.

Chapters 5, 6, and 7 review techniques for creating the structure, adding the details, and finishing the surface of a project. Each technique utilizes one or more tools in conjunction with one or more materials discussed in previous chapters. Chapter 8 puts it all together with a series of projects. Each project is created by the orderly and planned use of the right materials manipulated with the right tools according to the specific techniques that best apply to the unique requirements of each particular project.

My Wish List for the Use of This Book

I hope each reader first starts at the front cover and reads every word all the way through at least once. Then I hope the book will sit on each reader's worktable and become a much-used reference whenever a new project is contemplated—or when a previously started project isn't going well and needs to be rethought. I hope that every copy of this book gets filled with notes about what has worked and what hasn't, and what works better in a different set of circumstances. I hope that readers will develop their own set of worksheets following these outlines for new tools, materials, and techniques that they have discovered and become acquainted with. I strongly hope that readers will not view this book as a cookbook of recipes of how to build things, but rather that they will use the information in this volume as a springboard to find other creative ways of using and applying all that is in here. Finally, I hope readers will share all their discoveries with me so that I can include them in Volume 2!

CHAPTER 1 IDENTIFY: **Appearance Goals**
Function Goals

CHAPTER 2 ENSURE: **Safe Environment**

CHAPTER 3 SELECT: **Tools**
> Essentials—Eyes, hands, brain
> Cutters—knives, saws, scissors, cutting pliers
> Holders and joiners—pins, tape, adhesives, sewing machines
> Shapers—paintbrush, surform, sculpting tools, heat gun
> Applicators—#8 round brush, hot melt glue guns

CHAPTER 4 SELECT: **Materials**
> Adhesives—hot melt glue, white glue, spray adhesives
> Connectors—rings, springs, waxed thread, flexible tubing, Velcro
> Coatings—bronzing powder, pile fabric, flex screen, stretchy fabric, acrylic medium,
>   muslinlike fabrics, pigment, Sculpt or Coat®
> Fillings—batting, pellets
> Molding/sculpting—clay, latex, moulage, plaster, plaster bandage, thermoplastics
> Stiffeners/structure—backpack frame, boning, felt, foam, leather, stiff stuff, tubing, rod, wire
> Trim/decoration—balls, rope, leather, flexible rod, eyes, feathers, flowers, wheels

CHAPTER 5 APPLY: **Structure Techniques**
> Shape with round reed
> Shape with ethafoam plank
> Shape with fabric
> Create structure with casting latex in a negative mold
> Shape with thermoplastic mesh
> Shape with urethane foam
> Start with found shape

CHAPTER 6 APPLY: **Detail Techniques**
> Pad shape
> Place flex screen
> Rig moving parts
> Apply stiffener
> Sculpt details
> Apply connectors

CHAPTER 7 APPLY: **Surface Techniques**
> Cover the surface with fabric
> Paint color/texture on the surface
> Create dimension using color
> Soft sculpt details
> Add found object details

CHAPTER 8 PROJECTS: Appearance goals
> Function goals
> Tools
> Materials
> Structure technique(s)
> Detail technique(s)
> Surface technique(s)

Function and Appearance Goals

"The man is most original who can adapt from the greatest number of sources."

—Thomas Carlyle

The goal of a finished piece of theatre art is that it looks and performs the way it must in order to serve the play in the intended manner. Thus, the first step in the process is to identify your goal. The goal should be identified in terms of both:

1. **Function:** What it must be able to do and what, under any circumstances, it must not do. This is perhaps most important because it sets limits on the entire piece.
2. **Appearance:** What the finished item must look like.

Analyzing each component of the goal will help you determine all the parameters of the project. Collectively, these parameters will help you move through the rest of the steps of the processes of selecting the right tools, the right materials, and specific construction techniques for each project. By critically analyzing your goal for the project, you will have a much clearer picture of how to proceed.

Collecting the necessary information in order to define the goal for a given project should be accomplished with care, thoroughness, and attention to detail. You may need to research the art, life, and times of a particular population or person. You certainly need to consult the director, whose vision of the play needs to be reflected in everyone's work. You should consult the other members of the design team about the look, feel, and "flavor" of the rest of the objects and items on the stage with your piece. You may need to consult the stage manager and technical director about where a piece will fit and how it will move on and off the stage. You also must consult with any of the actors who will be involved with wearing and/or handling this piece. There will also be economic restrictions—time and money being chief among them. All this analysis is time well spent, since it will help you to reach your goal successfully the first time, rather than having to redesign and rebuild a piece in the final hours before opening night.

Close and careful examination of the goal determines the nature of the structure. It will indicate how the piece should be built, the tools and materials to be used, and the decorations needed to give the desired look. Once you know all about your destination, it then becomes possible to select the correct vehicle and the best route to travel in order to get there.

The diagnostic analysis of determining the structure begins with the center core—the frame. The most critical element in every construction project is the frame. Like the human body or a skyscraper, nothing else will function or look right if the skeleton (or foundation) and structure are wrong. If you start with the framework of the piece and get that right, the rest will fall into place much more easily and nicely than if you started any other way. When you determine what frame is needed, you have gone a long way toward determining the materials to be used. Based on what the shape is, decide if it needs to be hollow or filled, rigid or soft. Find the right materials and techniques with which to create the inner form based on your analysis of what you need as a finished product. Be certain your frame meets all the parameters, including movement. Is there room inside the frame for whatever or whomever to fit and manipulate the object successfully? Is the total object of a size that will fit into or through whatever it has to: doors, wings, rooms on the set, up to the flyloft? Is it light enough to move in the way it is supposed to? Is it strong enough to carry whatever it will have as an outside surface, and is it strong enough to interact with whatever else it will come in contact with and remain intact for as long as it needs to? Many of the pieces we build in my shop are for rental, so we tend to build them to last "forever." That is not always the case, and you have to weigh the cost of building for strength and durability against the reality of the specific circumstances you are dealing with.

Adding the details also helps to define the project—whether it's the features on a face, the clothing on a character, or the colors and textures chosen. Does the character have four fingers and a thumb on each hand or is it not quite that human, and should it have just three fingers to suggest more of an animal or otherworld creature? All the details need to be planned for at this stage so that there is adequate space and support provided in the structure.

Decorating the surface is also known as applying the "finishing touches." This final decoration can be compared to the frosting on a cake. A cake doesn't have the specific character it needs for its unique role—birthday, wedding, anniversary—until it is decorated, nor does it look as appealing without it.

Many will say that the appearance of the object is most important, for it is what the audience sees. Keep in mind, however, that we are dealing with art in a performance situation, and the way the object moves and how it interacts with its surroundings is just as important as the external appearance. If an Audrey II puppet (the man-eating plant from the musical *Little Shop of Horrors*) looks just fine on stage, but is made out of a material so heavy that the puppeteer cannot manipulate it, then the look doesn't work and the project will not be a success.

Applying the Approach to a Project: A Talking Tiger Rug

To illustrate the approach and make the problem-solving process more clear, let's take the talking tiger rug character from the recently revived musical *Me and My Girl*. (This rug is one of the projects shown in detail in Chapter 8.) Keep in mind that this show, *Me and My Girl*, is musical comedy at its silliest and that the period of the show is the early 1930s in England. The show takes place in and around the manor house of a wealthy landowner, and was intended as a spoof on British society and the importance of money and position in one's life. Its goal was to entertain and cheer people after the great financial crash of 1929. The scene we are concerned with is in the library of the manor house. The walls are lined with books and portraits of the various ancestors of this wealthy landowner. The ancestors come to life and tap-dance in their picture frames and later on-stage—but that's another project! There's a couch and perhaps another chair or two, and a tiger rug on the floor with the head downstage, facing the audience with eyes open and teeth bared. The actor must be able to sit on the floor of the stage next to this rug, talking to the rug while he surreptitiously slips his hand under and inside the head of this tiger and puppeteering it to look like it is speaking to him! The tiger's ears have to wiggle on cue, and then it gets whisked offstage by its tail.

So, our goal is a tiger with a three-dimensional head, artificial yet realistic eyes, bared teeth, and a full body skin stretched out on the floor. It must speak and wiggle its ears. Since it has to fly offstage, it cannot be heavy. It has to have jaw and ear mechanisms that are simple and foolproof since they are going to be manipulated by an actor who is primarily concerned with his own performance. The rug cannot break, tear, or fall apart since it needs to be intact to perform again next show. These appearance and function parameters guide the selection of materials, techniques of construction—both structure and detail—and techniques of decoration.

Ethafoam is used as the basic material for the head (see

Chapter 4 if you are not familiar with this kind of foam), because it is firm, strong, lightweight, and easily sculptable. Dowels are positioned so that a person's fingers and thumb can push and pull against them to make a speaking movement in the upper and lower jaws. The lower jaw is hinged with strips of leather. The shape of the face and head is sculpted before the ears go on. The ears are mounted on springs to allow movement and return to the original position when pulled with a cord to the inside of the mouth. Eyes, teeth, and nose are molded of a thermoplastic because of its moldability, its paintability with pigment in medium, and because its natural color is perfect for teeth. A dark red fabric covers the inside of the mouth, and white fur goes around the eyes. Fake tiger-striped fur covers the head and is cut long enough so that the rest can stretch out behind for the body.

Summary

Identifying the two components of the goal (function and appearance) is the essential first step of this problem-solving approach: what the item has to do and be, what it cannot do and be, and what it has to look like. Those elements define the overall shape, what the framework of the piece is, and how and with which materials and tools it is constructed. Decorating the surface is the final step. It is a very satisfying one, because by this time, you are so confident that your project will do and be exactly what it should that you can accomplish this final step with ease and pleasure!

Safety

"Education that does not first address health misses the heart of the matter."

—C. EVERETT KOOP, M.D.

D o not eat your arts and crafts materials." Everyone laughed, then realized that Val Kuehen, the speaker, was serious. How silly, I thought; then Val, who was presenting a workshop on creating three-dimensional forms of fiberglass for Macy's Thanksgiving Day parade, went on to explain how easy it was to leave your coffee and muffin on the workbench, do a little spray painting and a little gluing, get a layer of paint mist on the surface of your coffee and the glue on your fingertips; and then eat more of your muffin and drink the coffee!

You are an artisan.

You care about the quality of your materials and the quality of your work.

You want each object that you create to be the best it can be, because it reflects directly on you and your craft.

In order to be able to continue to do high quality work, you must take as much care of yourself and your environment (including your fellow workers) as you do of your materials and tools. You would not think of trying to sculpt a bust of clay in the dark—don't try to sculpt in a room with no ventilation. You wouldn't think of sewing silk with a burred needle—don't try to dye silk without wearing the right kind of protective gloves. You wouldn't drink coffee that had a visible layer of sawdust on top or a fly floating in it—don't spray paint near your beverage or your lunch where it can collect a more harmful yet invisible layer of paint particles and propellants.

There used to be a certain bohemian appeal of a "starving artist" who had pale skin, sunken chest, matted hair, paint under the fingernails, and nicotine stains on the fingers. While that extreme image is now somewhat déclassé, I continue to see people in our industry who are still harming themselves, unintentionally or otherwise. It is very easy to work on a sketch in charcoal and pastels, put them down, pick up a doughnut, lick the fingers clean of sugar, chalk, dye, and pencil erasings, and then swallow it all!

No safety program will be successful if each individual isn't attentive to the ongoing needs of their own body. Rest, sleep, clean air, food, and healthy skin are all essential if we are to sustain our ability to work over the years we have available, and to prevent burnout, acute or chronic illness, and injury. The deadline of dress rehearsal does not matter if the spray paint blows in your eyes and blinds you. Your creations this year may be lovely, but if you develop a chronic dermatitis or emphysema and cannot work beyond this year, then everyone loses.

Start Now

Since this is a guidebook for the craftsperson or theatre artisan, the safety focus in this book will be in terms of what you need to know and do in order to protect yourself. Now is the best possible time to establish your own personal protection program in order to assure yourself that you are working as safely as you can. It is not complicated, if you ask the following questions and heed their answers:

1. What are the internal hazards that I am exposed to?
2. What are the external hazards that I am exposed to?
3. How do I protect myself?
4. What can I use or do that is safer?

Internal Hazards

An "internal hazard" is one that is governed by one's own biological clock and rhythms. Being aware of what your body needs in order to work efficiently will allow you to gain control of your environment so you can utilize those situations that let you work at your best. Reflect on your work habits and body rhythms.

How much sleep do you need in order to function well?

How much more sleep do you need when you are under a lot of stress?

How much rest (rest being very different from sleep) do you need to be at your best?

How often do you need to take a break and for how long?

How often do you need to eat?

What are your personal physiological requirements that let you keep doing your best work? How much pressure do you need in order to get your creative juices really flowing?

How much more pressure does it take to really paralyze you so you can't work at all?

How can you best balance all these elements so that you don't end up totally fried by dress rehearsal?

Your work needs to be done in a safe, careful, and planned way. I am very fond of reminding my staff that *we do not have time to hurry*. When we do, we inevitably make mistakes that cost us in both time and materials; they can also result in a poorly made project, or worse, personal injury.

External Hazards

You can begin to identify the external hazards that you are exposed to by taking stock of all the materials, tools, and supplies with which you work. Make a list of each item and where you bought it. Contact your suppliers and ask for the MSDS (Material Safety Data Sheet) on each item that you get from each supplier. If they haven't heard of such a thing, assure them that the MSDS is required by federal law on all substances that may contain hazardous ingredients. If they do not have them for the items you have specified, they should obtain those sheets from the manufacturer. Or you can request the MSDS direct from the manufacturer. Be sure to request data sheets for all possible products that might contain any hazardous or toxic materials—paints, glues and adhesives, solvents, coatings, and sculptural materials are among the most common categories. Once you have collected all your MSDS, make a second copy of each. Store one copy of each in your office file for reference; store the other copy, in an organized way for easy and rapid access, in the work area near where you will use the potentially hazardous materials and near your protective supplies (respirators, fire extinguisher, gloves, dust masks, and the like).

Reading an MSDS for the first time can be a frightening experience, both for what it tells you that you do understand, and for what it tells you that you don't. Although these sheets may vary slightly in format or configuration, they are all similar to this sample, and they all must include the following categories of information:

- **Product identification:** includes the product manufacturer's name, address and emergency phone number, the chemical name, trade name, and chemical formula.

Material Safety Data Sheet

May be used to comply with
OSHA's Hazard Communication Standard,
29 CFR 1910.1200. Standard must be
consulted for specific requirements.

U.S. Department of Labor

Occupational Safety and Health Administration
(Non-Mandatory Form)

IDENTITY (As Used on Label and List)	Note: Blank spaces are not permitted. If any item is not applicable, or no information is available, the space must be marked to indicate that.

Section I

Manufacturer's Name	Emergency Telephone Number
Address (Number, Street, City, State, and ZIP Code)	Telephone Number for Information
	Date Prepared
	Signature of Preparer (optional)

Section II — Hazardous Ingredients/Identity Information

Hazardous Components (Specific Chemical Identity; Common Name(s))	OSHA PEL	ACGIH TLV	Other Limits Recommended	% (optional

Section III — Physical/Chemical Characteristics

Boiling Point		Specific Gravity (H_2O = 1)	
Vapor Pressure (mm Hg.)		Melting Point	
Vapor Density (AIR = 1)		Evaporation Rate (Butyl Acetate = 1)	

Solubility in Water

Appearance and Odor

Section IV — Fire and Explosion Hazard Data

Flash Point (Method Used)	Flammable Limits	LEL	UEL

Extinguishing Media

Special Fire Fighting Procedures

Unusual Fire and Explosion Hazards

Section V — Reactivity Data

Stability	Unstable		Conditions to Avoid
	Stable		

Incompatability *(Materials to Avoid)*

Hazardous Decomposition or Byproducts

Hazardous Polymerization	May Occur		Conditions to Avoid
	Will Not Occur		

Section VI — Health Hazard Data

Route(s) of Entry: Inhalation?   Skin?   Ingestion?

Health Hazards *(Acute and Chronic)*

Carcinogenicity: NTP?   IARC Monographs?   OSHA Regulated?

Signs and Symptoms of Exposure

Medical Conditions
Generally Aggravated by Exposure

Emergency and First Aid Procedures

Section VII — Precautions for Safe Handling and Use

Steps to Be Taken in Case Material Is Released or Spilled

Waste Disposal Method

Precautions to Be Taken in Handling and Storing

Other Precautions

Section VIII — Control Measures

Respiratory Protection *(Specify Type)*

Ventilation	Local Exhaust		Special	
	Mechanical *(General)*		Other	

Protective Gloves	Eye Protection

Other Protective Clothing or Equipment

Work/Hygienic Practices

- **Hazardous ingredients:** lists any ingredients within the product that can be hazardous. May also include information about the particular TLV (Threshold Limit Value) and PEL (Permissible Exposure Limit). Both terms express the amount of the ingredient that can safely be in the air during a normal workday.
- **Physical data:** gives important properties of the product or chemical, such as boiling point, appearance, and odor. This information indicated the degree of hazards associated with the product.
- **Fire and explosion hazard data:** gives the flash point— the temperature at which a chemical releases enough flammable vapor to catch fire. The proper method of extinguishing such a fire (CO_2, water, foam, etc.), and other fire or explosion hazards connected with the product is included in this section.
- **Health hazard data:** describes both acute and long-term effects of overexposure, emergency and first aid procedures, and medical conditions that might be aggravated by contact with the product.
- **Reactivity data:** indicates whether the product will react with other chemicals or conditions, such as burning or exploding, and how stable the product is chemically.
- **Spill or leak procedures:** tells how to manage a leak or spill, including types of cleanup and protective equipment needed, and the proper way to dispose of the product.
- **Special protection information:** lists types of protective equipment appropriate when working with the product.
- **Special precautions:** lists any special precautions to be taken when handling and storing the product.

The federal law is very specific when it comes to the information on an MSDS—*it has to be true*, so that you, the consumer, can believe what it says.

Awareness

If you find that your favorite glues, pigments, and other products have MSDSs that say they contain nasty things, that doesn't necessarily mean that you have to forsake them for a less effective product just because it is safer! It *does* mean that you are now enlightened and aware, and that is a very important step to take. We used to use a brush cleaner that was extraordinarily effective. It cleaned everything out of paint and makeup brushes. The container said it was nothing but toluene. That didn't mean much to us until we got the MSDS. If you don't know what it means, find out, because it appears fairly frequently on the MSDS sheets that we have, and you may be surprised which items of yours it appears in.

You've already taken the first step in dealing with hazardous substances: finding that they exist, and where and what they are. The next step is to determine what you have to do and what you have to have in order to protect yourself and your fellow workers and still safely use this product. You may decide that it is too much effort and abandon the product, but you may find that all it takes to protect you from a hazardous ingredient is to wear a respirator or a pair of impermeable gloves.

Protection

There are two basic ways to protect yourself. The best is to find a less toxic substitute. Failing that, you should find the correct means of protection from each harmful substance.

You take harmful substances into your body in three ways:

- **By *eating* them:** ingestion and digestion
- **By *touching* them:** absorption through the skin
- **By *breathing* them:** inhalation of airborne particles

The methods of protection vary with the route of entry of the substance into the body. Protection from *ingestion* of hazardous materials is perhaps the most basic and easiest to accomplish.

- Keep food and beverages away from your work area
- Wash your hands before eating, drinking, and smoking (if you still do that)
- Do not put nonfood articles in your mouth. This includes pins, tacks, pens, pencils, erasers, and your fingers (don't bite your nails!)
- Keep food, beverages, and cigarettes covered if you must have them in your work area at all

This may all sound simple, but think about it. How often do you put the end of a pen or pencil in your mouth to help you think? How often do you store a handful of pins or a threaded needle or a pencil between your teeth because it's a handy place to put something for just a minute? Often, these are unconscious or unthinking acts. Make a conscious effort to keep nonfood out of your mouth.

Protection from *absorption* of hazardous substances through the skin becomes a little more complicated because *you have to have the correct kind of protection* for each particular substance. Information about the type of protection necessary is included on the MSDS for each product, so be sure to check each specific MSDS for every product with which you come into contact. There are many different kinds of gloves made out of different materials. Be sure you know which will protect you from each product.

Protection from *inhalation* of airborne toxins is perhaps the most complicated of all. Again, your MSDS will give you the most reliable information on what kind of protection you need for which product. Please do not be foolish enough to say, as I have heard others say, "I'll just wear a respirator all the time and it will be okay." Wrong! Some respirators will not protect you from some substances. Not only do you need the right kind of respirator, you may need a specific kind of filter for that respirator. You will have to keep track of how long you have used each filter, and replace them before they become ineffective. Respirators need to fit properly in order to protect you. At least one major respirator manufacturer will send a representative to determine the correct style and measure for a proper fit for each person in that location at no charge. *Respirators are ineffective for a person with a beard.* Find the right tool for do each purpose and use it only for that purpose.

Legislated protection

We are all protected by federal legislation under the Occupational Safety and Health Act (OSHA) of 1970, which mandates that our workplaces have:

- an area for safe storage of toxic materials and supplies
- information readily accessible about those materials and their hazards
- equipment to protect us from materials that may be harmful to us
- a program of information for employees to learn about harmful materials and how to deal with them.

Much has been written about this law and its ramifications. A partial bibliography is included at the end of this book. Monona Rossol and Randall Davidson have both written and spoken extensively on the subject of safety in the theatre and their books are available in most libraries. There are numerous federal, state, local, and private agencies available to help employers establish and maintain a safe working environment for employees. *None of these will help if you do not personally care about yourself, your work, and your fellow workers.*

I urge each reader to become familiar with the OSHA regulations and to find out from your faculty or employer:

- Who is responsible for the safety program in your school or workplace
- Where information on toxic and hazardous materials (MSDS) is located
- Where the protective gear is stored, when it is used, for what purpose, and how it is cared for.

If you are unable to obtain answers to any of these questions, a pretty strong alarm should sound for you. Consider what steps you may need to take if there isn't a safety program in place. Offer to set one up. Offer to learn how to maintain a safe environment for yourself and your fellow workers. You will find a wealth of information and people willing to help, often for free. Start with your state Department of Labor, the office of Occupational Health Services, state Division of Public Health Services, or your local library.

Protection by choosing a safer alternative

While you are in the process of collecting your MSDSs, keep a list of the kinds of activities you use each item or substance for. Then cluster them into groups (you may use the groups I have identified for my list of materials later in this book, or develop your own). The idea is to group them according to function: adhesives, pigments (dyes and paints), coatings, molding materials, and the like. Review each MSDS in each group and rate them from most to least hazardous. You might want to develop a chart or matrix, or just keep a list. Whatever format you choose, *do this exercise* for your work environment! This information will be an invaluable resource for the materials you have on hand—what each is used for, how hazardous each one is, and most important, what the safer alternatives are. If there is an application for which you do not have a safe product, your imperative is to find one before the next time you need to use it.

There are two reasons why I have intentionally avoided

specific information about particular products and ingredients. First, products change frequently. The same product may appear with a new formula. The container reads "new and improved," which probably means that the manufacturer has either removed an ingredient that is harmful or no longer available, or has found others that are cheaper to include. Products are always changing, and anything included here is likely to be outdated by the time you read this. Second, and a more important reason, is that this chapter is intended to inspire the reader to think and act in a different way about safety; taking charge of learning about the substances you use is an important part of that. Take charge of this part of your craft. It is important that you become aware and enlightened about the hazards in your particular environment so that you can work as safely and intelligently as possible.

Tools

Q. Where did the term "pin money" originate?

A. For many centuries, pins, rather than sewn seams, were used to hold women's clothing together. The handmade pins, particularly brass ones, were so expensive that, in the late Middle Ages, English kings made the manufacture of pins a monopoly of the crown, permitting them to be sold only on the first two days of January. English husbands allowed their wives to put aside money for the annual sale. The phrase came later to mean any small amount of money saved by a frugal housewife for her own expenditures. The term is believed to have first appeared in print when Thomas Bacon wrote, "Marriage is out of the question unless the young lady has a small pin money purse of her own."

—*Boston Globe*, APRIL 26, 1995

There are enough tools available to fill an entire book; the ones included here are those I consider basic to the crafter's toolbox. Needles, thread, paper, scissors, pencils, chalk, rulers, tape measures, pins, and the like are used in all the traditional ways and are not mentioned again. The tools I have selected are either essential to every operation, are unusual, or are being used in a nontraditional way. I have also chosen to include them in basic groups, as types, as opposed to very specific tools of a particular size and shape. There will always be situations where you will need something special for a particular task (for example, a rhinestone setter or left-handed widget puller) and you will have to search until you find just the right tool for that job.

Tools fall into five categories:

1. **Essentials:** eyes, hands, brain
2. **Cutters:** knives, saws, scissors, cutting pliers
3. **Holders and joiners:** pins, tape, adhesives, sewing machines
4. **Shapers:** paintbrush, surform, sculpting tools, heat gun
5. **Applicators:** #8 round brush, hot melt glue guns

Each category is broken down into sections outlining a description of this group of tools, what their applications are, and techniques and precautions for these tools. No doubt, you will have or develop your own set of favorite tools for various uses. Whatever they are, don't forget to make full use of the essentials.

➤ Eyes
➤ Hands
➤ Brain

Description

Although, in theory, you always have these with you, you will be well served to consciously engage them each time you approach and work on a new project. Each of these tools needs to be fully active both during the planning phase of your work and during the actual creation of the object itself.

Application

Use your eyes not just to see what is here and now, but use them in all the ways they were meant to be used. Visualize the finished piece in your mind's eye; that way it becomes a goal you can see and therefore reach. Having this picture of the finished piece in your head will help you evaluate your progress toward your goal. Look at the materials you have to work with and picture them as you make them the right size and shape and begin to put them together. Then evaluate that progress in terms of your project goal. Use your eyes as evaluative tools with which to compare your progress with the visualized perfect finished product.

Your hands will also tell you a lot about how you are progressing. Feel whether your piece is smooth enough. Don't just look at it. Touch it! Feel whether a texture that is hard to see before it is painted is evenly distributed. Feel the inside of a place where your eyes can't reach and touch the contours you have just sculpted. See them with your hands in a different way from using your eyes. You will also use your hands in more conventional ways—to hold things together, to guide them into position, to use other tools—but don't forget the tactile pleasures of working with the tools and materials at your disposal.

Your brain is the original central computer and holds a lot of information. More important, it has the capacity for analytical thought. Use this essential tool all the time—become your own best critic and evaluator. Your brain can keep you on target as you progress through the steps of a project. If you let it be honest with you, it will guide you and not let you compromise any step along the way. Your brain will also give you signals about your health and safety. Pay attention to them, so that you are not hurt and so that your work becomes the best it can be. Learn to trust your judgment. Know when to stop because you are too tired, or when the glue is too hot, or you are too rushed. Pay attention to all the warnings, and accommodate them so your project will not be hindered. If you are running out of time and are overtired and stressed, let your brain figure out a way to stop. Get a little rest, and then bring the work to completion—perhaps not with all the detail you had originally wanted, but in a safe and satisfactory way. This is your brain's job and you can benefit from letting it do this work rather than overriding those important messages and pushing through to an unsatisfactory finish.

Techniques and Precautions

Care of your essential tools is as essential as the tools themselves. You must rest your brain, you must not cut or burn your hands, and you must protect and rest your eyes. If you don't, you will not be able to continue your work without having to accommodate either a temporary or permanent injury and its consequences. Loss of time to work on a project that inevitably has a deadline, or loss of the use of eyes or hands, even temporarily, can have a great negative impact on you, your fellow workers, and the entire production.

- ➤ Craft knives:
  X-Acto, matte

- ➤ Serrated knife

- ➤ Saws:
  jig-
  hand-
  band

- ➤ Scissors:
  many sizes

- ➤ Cutting pliers

Description

Used, as the name implies, to cut, score, sculpt, or otherwise make smaller pieces out of larger pieces; use with care—if you don't, you may hurt yourself!

Application

Craft knife: Good for cutting paper, sculpting small details in ethafoam, plaster

Serrated or wavy-edged knife: Buy an inexpensive one so you can replace it when it gets dull; good for cutting ethafoam

Saw: Jig- or band saw useful for rigid foams like ethafoam and insulation foam; handsaw good for cutting lengths of CPVC

Scissors: Large ones are especially good for cutting sheets of urethane foam and thermoplastic mesh

Cutting pliers: Used to cut millinery wire, some cord

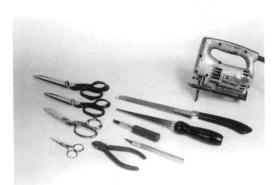

Techniques and Precautions

- Keep them sharp
- Protect the blades from knicks and bumps
- A dull or rusty blade will do as much to hinder your project as a sharp one will to help your project to a satisfactory completion

HOLDERS AND JOINERS

Description

These tools hold or join parts together. Holders such as pins, tape, and clothespins will hold parts together temporarily, either while glue sets, or while you run the parts through the sewing machine. Joiners connect parts in a more permanent manner. Adhesives and sewing machines are joiners. (See Applicators for a discussion about glue guns.)

> ➤ Pins
> ➤ Gaffer's tape
> ➤ Clothespins
> ➤ Adhesives
> ➤ Sewing machine with zigzag feature
> ➤ Overlock sewing machine
> ➤ Quick links

Application

My rule about joining is that if parts can be sewn, they should be. *Never glue or tape what you can sew.* You can always undo sewing. Not only is it close to impossible to undo gluing, you are then left with the mess of glue on your fabric. My second rule is that if gluing is your method of choice, especially with rigid parts, use a second method of joining to augment, such as tape or wire.

Pins: Hold parts in place until they can be joined, or temporarily mark a place where a part will be joined later

Gaffer's tape: Holds ethafoam parts together and in place while hot melt glue sets. May be used as a secondary joiner in connection with hot glue

Clothespins: Hold parts, especially millinery wire, in place while hot melt glue is applied and until it sets

Adhesives: Range from white glue to sticks of hot melt adhesive. Hot melt glue stick sizes range from small to large. The very tiny ones are for use with small glue guns and have a relatively low melting temperature and are good for jewelry and other small, lightweight objects. A medium-sized glue stick (such as you get at a hardware store) comes both as a clear, lower temperature stick and amber-colored sticks, which require a hotter temperature and will give a stronger bond, as with wood and heavier objects. We use a special-shaped tan stick, which requires a heavier glue gun for our large projects. Made by 3M, it is a pretty high temperature

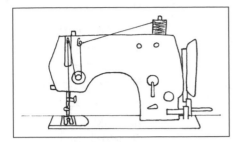

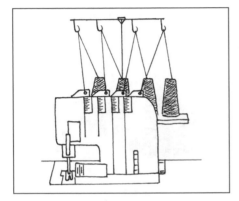

glue, is quite expensive, and takes a special-shaped gun, but if you do a lot of this work it's a great investment. See also a discussion of adhesives as a material in the next chapter.

Sewing machine with zigzag feature: Very handy for sewing millinery wire to fabric. Stitch slowly and carefully, bending the wire along the shape you want it to be as you go along. Zigzag back and forth many times over both ends (which should be overlapped about 5/8 of an inch) to keep them from poking out.

Overlock sewing machine: This machine (generally with four or five threads compared to a three-thread machine) can sew a seam stitch and bind the edges of a fabric at the same time, giving a very strong seam.

Quick links: Handy holders, found in hardware stores, that come in various sizes. Shaped like a link, it has elongated nut that screws open and close.

Techniques and Precautions

- Keep all holders and joiners clean and free of excess glue and paint
- *Always* close safety pins before putting down or in a container, so that the next person along doesn't get hurt

SHAPERS

Description

These tools help form the shape of some objects

Application

Paintbrush: Use for applying a texturing material in medium; also for applying pigment in such a way as to create dimension with color

Surform: A wonderful type of sculpting or shaping tool, whose blade has a "grater" type surface with multiple small curved blades. It can scrape away small, even amounts of a semisoft material, such as ethafoam

Orangewood stick / sculpting tool: This tool is best used to create fine details in soft, moldable clays and thermoplastics

Hair dryer / heat gun: These tools are useful for drying wet materials, such as plaster bandage, and for softening thermoplastic mesh. When thermoplastic mesh is softened, it can be shaped and will stick to itself. Decorative objects, Velcro, and other items can be bonded to it.

➤ Paintbrush
➤ Surform
➤ Orangewood stick / sculpting tool
➤ Hair dryer / heat gun

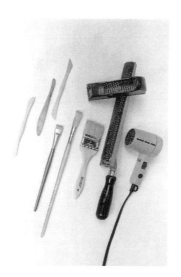

Techniques and Precautions

- **Paintbrush:** Always clean bristles thoroughly. Hang up to dry by the handle, bristles down, to prolong the life of the brush. I prefer to buy either very good brushes that I will care for and use for years, or very inexpensive ones that I can use and throw away
- **Surform:** Replace blades often for best results
- **Orangewood stick / sculpting tool:** Keep clean and free of sculpting material
- **Hair dryer / heat gun:** Don't hold hair dryer too close to object being heated since it will overheat and shut off. If heat gun has a metal nozzle that directs the heat, place only on a nonflammable surface until the hot parts of the gun cool

➤ #8 round brush
➤ glue guns

Description

These are used to apply a material to other materials

Application

A **#8 round brush** is a natural hair bristle brush with a round ferrule used to apply liquid latex. It is not particularly expensive and is generally obtainable from theatrical make-up suppliers. When in use, keep the bristles moistened with liquid soap in water anytime you are not brushing with it, in order to prevent the latex from drying and building up on the bristles. Each time you are going to paint with it, remove it from the soapy water, blot on a little pad of folded paper toweling, then dip in the liquid latex, and away you go!

Glue guns are almost a household word these days, but the range of available sizes may not be. The very small ones take clear, mini glue sticks, and are often used in making jewelry and very small objects. They do not get very hot (compared to the standard ones you find in hardware stores for carpentering) and the glue does dry clear. At the other end of the spectrum is an industrial-strength treasure manufactured by 3M. This gun is orange, takes sticks that are thicker than usual, are amber-colored, and melt at a higher temperature than standard variety. The housing of the gun has a tapered peg about an inch long molded into each side that allows you to rest the gun safely on your workbench without the tip burning anything. There are a number of accessories available for this model, such as different applicator tips, a squeeze grip, and the like.

Techniques and Precautions

- **#8 round brush:** See the previous section for care of paintbrushes
- **Glue gun:** There are two tips to keep in mind: 1. Keep the plug end of the electrical cord healthy. Check that all three prongs (yes, the hotter guns, at least, should be grounded) are firm in the plug and are parallel to each other (like when new). Be sure that the other end of the cord is secure in the gun itself and that there are no bare wires anywhere there or along the length of the

cord. 2. Keep the tip clean of excess glue and other bits of frimfram that it will pick up along the way. The easiest way to do this is to unplug the gun and wipe the tip with a clean piece of rag after the tip has cooled down enough to touch safely. Do not use a paper towel as it will stick, may burn, and make a worse mess.

CHAPTER FOUR

Materials

"The chances of success of a particular project are greater if the craftsperson is aware of and open to considering all the possibilities available."

—Ann Carnaby

This chapter discusses many of the materials available to us craftspeople. They have been grouped according to categories that best identify their most common function. This is not meant to be an exhaustive list; rather, it should suggest to you some of the possible ways to use the materials, and what types to look for:

Adhesives

Connectors

Coatings

Fillings

Molding / sculpting

Stiffeners / structure

Trim / decoration

I have described each material in terms of its degree of hazard: as either "nontoxic" or "use with precautions." This is not an official rating and it refers to more than just hazardous materials. I avoid using materials that are hazardous. I firmly believe that we should all make a conscious effort to avoid the things we know are harmful and get in the habit of using materials that, to the best of our knowledge, will be less harmful or will not hurt us.

I have also included basic information about each material, such as a description of what it is, how it can be used, points to consider either when using (or deciding to use) the material, and special techniques and ways of handling it when they apply. Sources and cost have been expressed only in the most general of terms, since that information may vary widely in different geographic areas and over time. I have identified each material as either inexpensive, moderate, or costly, just to give the reader some notion of where a particular material fits relative to other items of the same type.

A section for each material called Techniques and Precautions includes protective steps related to hazardous material when applicable, but also describes general precautions or care to be taken. Some are expressed as warnings and have to do with the nature of the material itself, such as "this will fray quickly when cut," so that those using this particular material for the first time will know what to expect.

The information in this chapter cannot be all-inclusive. The remarks here are meant simply to guide you in making more effective choices.

HOT MELT GLUE

Hazard Rating: Use with precautions

Description: Adhesive in stick form applied with a gun. Sticks supplied in varying lengths and thicknesses, or in pellets. Available from hardware and craft stores; prices range depending on type and quantity: generally inexpensive.

Application

- Most successful on pieces that do not bend or flex
- Bonds most surfaces, even those with minimum porosity

Techniques and Precautions

- Feed stick into gun, plug gun in, follow directions
- May also melt sticks in a nonstick pan over a burner or electric pan to get a soft paste that can be spread with a knife or stick
- Keep hands over or to the side of the work—excess melted glue will fall straight down
- If melted glue falls on skin, *do not put it off*. Leave it in place and submerge glue and skin in cold water immediately

Hazard Rating: Nontoxic

Description: White viscous water-soluble adhesive (Elmer's and Mighty Tacky are two brand names). Available from hobby, stationery, or craft stores; inexpensive.

Application

Joins most porous substances, such as cloth, paper, wood, for which it is safe and useful. It will also bond pigments and porous fabrics (such as lightweight cotton) to a nonporous material (such as an ethafoam plank or rod), making it possible to texture or color the material

Techniques and Precautions

- Use normal safety precautions
- Use full strength or dilute with water

Hazard Rating: Use with precautions

Description: Adhesive in a spray can. Supplied in various sizes with different sized and shaped nozzles. Available from hobby, craft, and hardware stores; moderate cost.

Application

Apply a thin even coat to bond layers together, such as fabric over foam

Techniques and Precautions

- Protect areas surrounding part to receive adhesive as the spray will cover a wide area. Use an open box for small items. Use outdoors whenever possible
- Make sure there's adequate ventilation
- Read instructions on can for any specific protective measures

Hazard Rating: Nontoxic

Description: Metal or plastic, round or D-shaped, split, overlapping, or whole; made in a wide variety of sizes and materials. Available at hardware, craft, and sewing stores; inexpensive.

Application

- Useful wherever you need to provide a little "handle" on the end of a cord, or to weight an object
- Use two D rings as a temporary closure

Techniques and Precautions

- Metal rings tend to be heavier, so they will hang from the cord they're tied to, and may be easier to find
- Rings may be sewn directly onto an object. Using a tab folded around the ring is often stronger and may be more decorative
- Use normal safety precautions

Hazard Rating: Nontoxic

Description: A coil of wire that, when stretched, will return to its original size with a force proportionate to its size and strength. Available in a wide variety of sizes, diameters, and strengths from hardware and craft stores; inexpensive.

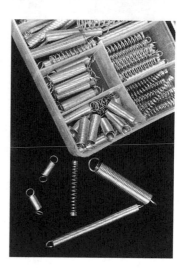

Application

Used for closing things automatically, or returning something to its original position

Techniques and Precautions

- Select right size and strength for project
- Be careful; they can pinch

Hazard Rating: Nontoxic

Description: Thread that has been treated with wax to make it slippery (Silamide is a brand name). Comes in a variety of colors and, from one manufacturer, is supplied on a narrow cardboard bolt (see photo). Available from major suppliers of sewing room equipment; moderate cost.

Application

- Hand sewing of any type of closure
- Stronger than regular thread for hand sewing, but not as strong as button twist
- Doesn't tangle

Techniques and Precautions

- Use normal safety precautions
- When supplied on the cardboard bolt, remove the perforated end of outside sleeve and cut throughout all the exposed loops of thread; you will then have lengths that remain protected and untangled
- Pull one thread at a time through the window for use

Hazard Rating: Nontoxic

Description: Plastic or Teflon tubing usually sold by the foot off a roll from hardware stores; inexpensive to moderate cost.

Application

Use to provide smooth passage for cord used to manipulate a moving part

Techniques and Precautions

- Attach by wrapping tube at the point of each attachment with muslin, then hot gluing the muslin to the other surface
- May spray inside of tubing with silicone spray to assure smooth passage of cord
- Use normal safety precautions

HOOK-AND-PAD TAPE

Velcro

Hazard Rating: Nontoxic

Description: Tape woven with one side having tiny hooks on surface and the other having a "woolly" pad on the surface. When placed together, the hook side clings to the pad side and the two stick together. Available by the yard and as small pieces ("buttons") in various widths and colors, with and without adhesive backing, from notions and sewing suppliers and hardware stores; moderately expensive method for connecting parts.

Application

Use whenever quick-opening is required, as in breakaway costumes

Techniques and Precautions

- Only useful as a temporary closure, as a strong tug will pull this connector apart
- Not as reliable a closure as buttons, hooks and eyes, bars, or even most snaps, but can be useful for specific applications
- Is usually noisy when pulled apart

Hazard Rating: Use with precautions

Description: Finely milled metallic powder. Usually supplied in one-ounce, four-ounce, and one-pound containers from theatrical and craft supply stores; moderate cost.

Application

Use to give a metallic appearance to a non-metal surface

Techniques and Precautions

- Make small piles of bronzing powder and binder (either medium or diluted Sculpt or Coat®) next to each other on dish or palette
- Mix only as much as you will brush on at one time
- To give depth to a piece, brush on a mixture of medium mixed with a texturing material like sand or cornmeal and let dry; paint the piece black; then dry-brush bronzing powder over so that some of the black still shows
- Gives a very heavy metal look
- Can be painted or stencilled onto fabric or yarn for a metallic look
- Use a dust mask

Hazard Rating: Nontoxic

Description: Fabric, woven or knit, with fibers uniformly rising from one surface to simulate fur or to give texture to the surface, as in velvet or corduroy; Vellux (a brand name of a fuzzy blanket material) has pile on both sides. Supplied by the yard from fabric stores; moderate cost.

Application

Use to cover a structure and create a soft, fuzzy surface, as when creating an animal

Techniques and Precautions

- Cut edges often don't fray
- Conceals precise shape of structure underneath, so detailing of understructure is often not critical
- Use normal safety precautions

FLEX SCREEN

Hazard Rating: Nontoxic

Description: Flexible screening intended for windows and doors. Available in various widths, sold by the foot from hardware stores; moderate cost.

Application

- Cover eye and mouth openings in walkabout parade costumes and larger-than-life-sized puppets
- Use as a scrim
- Use as a stiffener inside sleeve puffs, bustle ruffle, or crinoline

Techniques and Precautions

- Can be painted on outside with detailing of eyeball or tongue
- To get a slight curve to eye, place on inside of head, push through eye opening as far as possible without causing screen to pucker, then hot glue in place
- Bind edges with twill tape or seam binding when using on the inside of a parade head, so there are no sharp ends to hurt the wearer

Hazard Rating: Nontoxic

Description: One- or two-way stretch fabric, knit of a variety of fibers; can have pile (such as stretch velour), or loopy texture (such as stretch terry cloth). Supplied by the yard, often milled fifty to sixty inches wide; from fabric stores; ranges in price from inexpensive to moderate, depending on fiber content.

Application

Stretch to cover an object with contours; Lycra has good two-way stretch and strength

Techniques and Precautions

- Drape over object to be covered and pin where seams need to be. Remove from object to stitch seams on an overlock machine that will accommodate the stretchiness of the fabric
- Use normal safety precautions

Hazard Rating: Nontoxic

Description: Coating, sealer, binder, vehicle for pigment and texturing materials. Available in one-gallon pails from theatrical supply stores; smaller containers can be found in art and hobby stores; moderate cost.

Application

- Add pigment, bronzing powder, texturing material to apply to porous or nonporous surfaces
- Use to waterproof surfaces

Techniques and Precautions

- Place a small amount of medium and pigment or texturing material next to each other on dish
- Mix only as much as will be used in each brushful at a time
- To give depth to the surface of a piece, brush on a mix of medium and sand or cornmeal; let it dry, paint it black or another dark color; then dry-brush bronzing powder or pigment over top so that some of the under-color is still visible
- Can be painted or stencilled onto fabric or yarn to give a metallic look
- Use normal safety precautions

Hazard Rating: Nontoxic

Description: Usually natural cotton fabric, from gauze to canvas, woven in various weights. Osnaburg is an unbleached cotton "rag" fabric that shrinks unevenly when washed and dried; gauze is thin and loosely woven. Sold by the yard by theatrical supply houses and fabric stores; moderate cost.

Application

Gives interesting texture for "rough" unfinished garments

Techniques and Precautions

- Machine wash and dry several times before cutting to get maximum texture and shrinkage
- Use normal safety precautions

Hazard Rating: Nontoxic

Description: Moist, concentrated color, to be diluted with water and/or water and a binder. Casein pigments can be purchased in quart or gallon containers from theatrical supply stores (some colors may be available in five-gallon containers). Acrylic paints come in small tubes or bottles from art supply stores. Casein pigment is less expensive than acrylic, which is moderate.

Application

When you want to paint a color on a surface

Techniques and Precautions

- Casein pigment in water is fine for painting on porous surfaces, such as muslin or other fabric and wood; when supplied for scenic painting they are the least expensive because they do not contain the binder that latex and acrylic paints have, and are often the most pure colors
- Mix casein pigment with a binder, such as flat or gloss acrylic medium, if applying pigment to a nonporous surface, or if the object needs to be waterproofed
- Casein pigments will spoil after a period of time and emit an awful smell
- Acrylic pigments are easy to obtain and safe to use, but are more expensive in larger quantities

SCULPT OR COAT®

Hazard Rating: Nontoxic

Description: Thick, plasticlike water-based cream that gives strength to a piece and adheres objects to metal, wood, or fabric; dries clear unless a pigment or colorant is added. Supplied in one- and five-gallon pails from theatrical supply stores; moderate cost.

Application

- Strengthens paper, Styrofoam hats, glass objects
- Imbed hair (or other material) into it for texturing
- Attaches "jewels"
- Good binder and strengthener for ceramics
- Good as a transparent weave filler

Techniques and Precautions

- Use two coats for added strength, applying each coat in a different direction
- To strengthen a glass object, use a layer of cream, then a layer of gauze, then another layer of cream
- Put in a plastic bag, cut a hole, and squeeze out as you would with a cake frosting bag for raised decoration
- Can add pigment and/or water to change color and consistency
- Full-strength use gives more of a surface shine than when thinned with water
- A thinner consistency has a faster drying time
- Warm water aids dissolving
- Can be painted over using latex or enamel paints
- Use normal safety precautions

Hazard Rating: Nontoxic

Description: Synthetic fiber filling (such as sometimes used in quilting) is relatively lightweight and has moderate movement and flexibility; cotton batting is quite heavy; Dacron fill is much stiffer (it's used in upholstery), so the loft won't compress as much as others. Supplied as sheets, in rolls, or bagged in bulk. Available from hobby, craft, and upholstery supply stores; relatively inexpensive.

Application

- Batting or sheet polyfill is used for body padding and stuffing
- It is also useful when you want to create a smooth, rounded, or soft-looking surface over a frame that has ribs or other contours that shouldn't show

Techniques and Precautions

- Layer for body padding
- Stitch each layer to base, otherwise it may shift or bunch
- Pack loose for soft, squishy feel; pack full for firm feel
- Cotton batting is very heavy and is not washable
- Synthetic fibers are better to use for most projects as they are highly washable

Hazard Rating: Nontoxic

Description: Birdseed, dried peas, beans, Styrofoam pellets, popcorn. Supplied in various forms from food stores and packaging supply stores; inexpensive.

Application

- Fill for soft-sculpted objects, bean bags, body padding (especially breasts, as in the aging stripper costume)
- Especially useful when you need to create movement
- The heavier the pellets, the greater the independent movement the object will have

Techniques and Precautions

- Simulates lifelike movement, responds to gravity
- Leakage is not usually harmful, just a nuisance
- May be noisy so watch body microphones

CLAY—AIR-DRYING

Hazard Rating: Nontoxic

Description: Air- or household oven–drying clays for sculpture. Celluclay is the brand name of an instant papier-mâché, and DAS is the brand name of a very nice air-drying clay from Europe. Both products are packaged in various sizes by weight and are available from hobby and craft suppliers; relatively inexpensive.

Application

Use for sculpting shapes and positive molds

Techniques and Precautions

- Work as with any clay, with minimum kneading required
- Celluclay, the instant papier-mâché, is supplied dry; you must add water to it; it dries to a coarse texture and can be sanded, but fine details are tricky to produce
- DAS is more claylike: You must keep it moist while working it or it will harden; you can get fine details; it has fibers for strength and it can be sanded smooth and painted
- Use normal safety precautions

Hazard Rating: Nontoxic

Description: Modeling clay that stays soft. Supplied in sticks by the box, in a variety of colors. Available from stationery and art supply stores; inexpensive and reusable.

Application

Use as a temporary sculpt for making negative plaster mold; plasticine never hardens so it can be remodeled countless times. It also has a certain amount of adhesive quality to it—for example, I use a blob of it under the base of each window candle at Christmastime to hold them in place on very narrow windowsills. When I take the candles down, I just wad the bits of plasticine together and put them in a baggie for the next year.

Techniques and Precautions

- Sculpt desired positive out of plasticine and make plaster negative—pull plasticine out when plaster is set
- Use normal safety procedures

CASTING LATEX

Slush Latex

Hazard Rating: Use with precautions

Description: Milky liquid rubber, which has some impurities and a strong ammonia odor. Supplied in one- and five-gallon pails from theatrical supply stores; moderate cost.

Application

Use for hollow rubber noses and other prosthetics

Techniques and Precautions

- Pigment can be added to liquid before it is cast
- Color darkens when dry
- Add filler to liquid for a harder piece when dry
- Pour into plaster negative molds (no need for a release); let it set until desired thickness (it cures from plaster inward); pour off excess liquid; let inner surface dry; powder with talc, then pull from mold
- Add layers of gauze in semiset layer of latex for greater strength. Pour excess latex out before desired thickness is obtained, then add a layer of gauze, letting latex set, then add another layer of latex either by pouring or painting in; repeat process until desired strength and thickness
- Latex can be cut with scissors
- Watch eyes and skin for reaction to ammonia and for latex sensitivity

MOULAGE

Alginate

Hazard Rating: Nontoxic

Description: Gelatinous material which, when melted to a liquid, can be poured over almost anything to cast a negative mold of that object. Supplied in one-pound bags or jars from theatrical makeup suppliers; moderate cost.

Application

Mainly used for creating plaster positive molds; although alginate is most often used for life masks, it can be used whenever you need to take a negative impression to create a positive plaster reproduction. Dentists use a finer grade of this to make impressions of patients' teeth.

Techniques and Precautions

- Melt in double boiler, stirring slowly till smooth—do not stir quickly as it will create bubbles that are hard

to get out and will destroy the surface of the mold; let it cool slightly, then scoop or pile with hands or ladle onto object being cast
- Be sure to get moulage into all tiny undercuts and crevices
- Coat outside with plaster bandage to prevent hardened moulage from breaking when being removed from object
- If moulage is the reusable type, after plaster mold is made, break moulage into pieces similar in size to when it was new
- Store in airtight container to maintain moistness
- Dilute with water if it gets too thick
- See life mask project for precautions when casting a person's face

Hazard Rating: Nontoxic

Description: Dry plaster powder for mold making. Available in twenty-five-, fifty-, and one-hundred-pound bags from theatrical supply houses; inexpensive.

Application

- Used for life masks and negative plaster molds
- Is stronger than, and produces finer detail, than plaster of paris

Techniques and Precautions

- Use the following ratios of plaster to water:
  Hydrocal: 44 parts water to 100 parts dry plaster by weight
  Ultracal: 38 parts water to 100 parts dry plaster by weight
- Always add plaster to water, not the other way around
- Never add more water than specified above; if mix is too dry, throw it away and start again; add powder slowly, let it absorb the water, then stir gently (stirring vigorously will produce bubbles that will distort final mold)
- Can be used in an alginate negative or over a clay positive without a release
- Can be used plaster-to-plaster only with a release, such as petroleum jelly
- Any cement powder can be very drying to skin so handle with care and/or use rubber gloves

PLASTER BANDAGE
Rigid Wrap

Hazard Rating: Nontoxic

Description: Plaster-impregnated gauze bandage. Supplied in four-inch- and eight-inch-wide rolls from hobby, craft, and theatrical supply stores; inexpensive.

Application

Use for mask making and for coating and texturing an object

Techniques and Precautions

- May use plaster bandage over an existing mask or other object to alter shape or texture
- Allows you to create a mask directly on a person's face
- Use a thin layer of petroleum jelly or oil over eyebrows, eyelashes, and facial hair if placing plaster bandage directly on a person's face

THERMOPLASTICS

Friendly plastic, Varaform, Hexcelite

Hazard Rating: Nontoxic

Description: Ivory-colored plastic, which softens when heated and hardens when returned to room temperature; supplied as a solid pellet or sheet of plastic, or as plastic impregnated onto a mesh fabric of various sizes. The natural color is ivory but sheet colors vary for craft projects; mesh is also available in different sizes. Available from craft, hobby, and some theatrical supply houses; relatively expensive, but there is little waste.

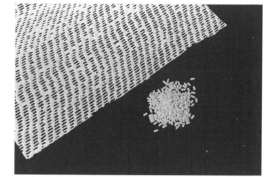

Application

Solid pellets can be formed into rigid items, such as teeth or buttons; mesh can be used to form and drape small and medium shapes. The fact that it softens and looses its shape at a relatively low temperature may limit its usefulness

Techniques and Precautions

- Soften in bath of heated water over electric burner (impregnated mesh may be softened with a hair dryer)
- Remove from bath with stick or tongs
- Form with hands or sculpting tools
- Be careful that you don't get burned!
- Do not expose mesh piece to heat (either from sun or stage lights) as it will soften and lose its sculpted shape

BACKPACK FRAME

Hazard Rating: Use with precautions

Description: Hollow, lightweight aluminum (or other metal) frame for a canvas or nylon backpack. Be sure you select a complete frame that can be removed from the pack, not one that depends on the pack for part of its structure. Available from sporting goods and department stores; frames vary in price from moderate to expensive, depending on style and strength of frame.

Application

Interior support for a large structure with a person inside (either for a puppet or an object that is very tall or cumbersome). Giant puppets are the most logical application, but we also have had occasion to use them for a ski show (see Elephant, Lion, and Tiger projects) when a dinosaur on skis was wanted. It provided the support for a twelve-foot-tall dinosaur while permitting a single skier to use his arms freely inside for balance.

Techniques and Precautions

- Extenders may be put inside uprights to make the frame taller or added perpendicularly to make the frame wider
- Take care not to overload the frame with either too much balanced weight, or an unbalanced, uneven weight that would strain back, neck, or leg muscles

Hazard Rating: Nontoxic

Description: Flexible foam commonly used in upholstery. Available in varying sizes of sheets or lengths in rolls, with various thicknesses (one-half, one, and two inches are the most common). Sold by upholstery and foam rubber suppliers; inexpensive.

Application

Use to form structure under an outer fabric for a walkabout costume or other soft-sculpted piece

Techniques and Precautions

- Use fabric and foam adhesive on both edges being glued and press together
- Cover surface with fabric (stretchy or pile)
- Use normal safety precautions with adhesives

RIGID FOAM

Ethafoam

Hazard Rating: Use with precautions

Description: Firm, closed cell foam. An ethafoam plank looks similar to Styrofoam, but is more dense and stronger; it can be sculpted to an almost smooth surface and is especially lightweight for its strength. Supplied in planks measuring two feet by eight feet by two inches from manufacturers (Acme Foam, 3M, among others) and suppliers of industrial packaging materials; expensive.

Application

Puppetry, oversized parade heads

Techniques and Precautions

- Cut with serrated knife, handheld jigsaw, or band saw
- Sculpt with smaller knife or surform
- May coat with Sculpt or Coat®, then sand for a hard, smooth surface
- Cutting with a heat knife releases fumes—it's safer to cut with regular knife or saw
- Sculpting with a surform releases dust particles so use a dust mask

Hazard Rating: Nontoxic

Description: Poly boning is a strip of plastic in a pellon (nonwoven fabric) casing; Rigilene boning comprises several strips of plastic in a woven casing; steel boning comprises sprung steel in a buckram or plastic casing. Boning is supplied by the yard or by the piece, in various widths and materials. Available from sewing and notions suppliers; moderate cost.

Application

- Dress bodices and corsets
- Structured undergarments
- Hoop petticoats

Techniques and Precautions

- Plastic boning is not as stiff or strong as steel boning
- Plastic boning is suitable for light- to medium-weight garments where some stiffness is desired
- Machine stitch casing, which sticks out on either side of a central channel that houses the plastic stiffener, into garment
- Steel boning is more suitable for hoops in petticoats or other projects that require extra strength
- Use normal safety precautions

Hazard Rating: Nontoxic

Description: Nonwoven fabric of varying thicknesses and fibers; not as strong as woven fabric. Supplied by the yard and in precut squares. Available from fabric and crafts stores; inexpensive to moderate.

Application

Reinforcing for thickness, shape, and strength

Techniques and Precautions

- May be painted or glued
- Use normal safety precautions

Hazard Rating: Nontoxic

Description: Animal skin, without fur, cured for use as garments, shoes, accessories (if fur remains it's referred to as a pelt). Usually supplied by the skin from leather supply stores; expensive.

Application

To create a structure, traditionally used for foot coverings and accessories; also useful whenever a soft, flexible part is needed

Techniques and Precautions

- When sewing or repairing fur pelts, hand sew the edges flush together with herringbone stitches; then cover seam on inside (nonfur side) with twill tape or seam binding held on with rubber cement for strength
- When sewing leather, to get a less bulky seam, overlap the seam allowances, wrong side to right side, and stitch either by hand or machine. Use a "leather" needle, which has a triangular-shaped shaft as opposed to a round one and pierces a dense skin more easily for easier sewing
- Use normal safety precautions

Hazard Rating: Nontoxic

Description: Woven fabric inherently stiff even after repeated washings. Supplied by the yard; available at fabric stores; moderate cost.

Application

Use as an interfacing to stiffen an object or garment

Techniques and Precautions

- Use like you would any interfacing
- Use normal safety precautions

Hazard Rating: Nontoxic

Description: May be made of plastic (CPVC) or metal (copper, aluminum). Supplied by the foot and in various diameters at building, hardware, and plumbing supply stores; plastic is inexpensive, copper is expensive.

Application

- Use for structural framework to give strength and rigidity inside another material that will give shape to the object
- Use for inner supports or handles

Techniques and Precautions

- Be certain to have the correct adhesive for joining pieces; it's usually available from the same source as the tubing
- Be sure to get the MSDS on the adhesive
- If you've selected plastic tubing for your project, buy CPVC (pipe for cold water), because it is less expensive than pipe made to carry hot water
- Use normal safety precautions with adhesive

Hazard Rating: Nontoxic

Description: Wooden dowel of various diameters (the smallest sizes are toothpicks or bamboo, the larger sizes are closet poles). Available by the foot or precut length from food, hardware, and lumber stores; inexpensive.

Application

- Used often in puppetry to span the interior space of a puppet
- Used as either a brace for the puppeteer's fingers or, in larger puppets, a larger size is used to lift and manipulate parts of the puppet
- Provides interior bracing or strengthening

Techniques and Precautions

- When gluing dowel or pole to ethafoam, surround the end of the dowel with a layer of ethafoam (either square or round) so that the hot glue may be applied both to the surface of the dowel and the surrounding ethafoam, and then to the bottom of both materials to give a larger surface, making a stronger bond
- Use normal safety precautions with hot glue

WIRE

Hazard Rating: Nontoxic

Description: Millinery wire, which is thread-wrapped wire and supplied on a bolt; coat hanger wire. Available from millinery and notions suppliers; inexpensive to moderate.

Application

Reinforce and strengthen edges of hats and crowns. NOTE: Because wire will retain whatever shape you give it, you should not use it with materials that will later be bent into other shapes, such as in garments. It's ideally suited for hats and masks

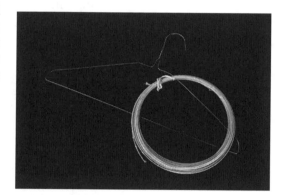

Techniques and Precautions

- Sew to edge of felt, leather, or fabric part with hand stitch or machine zigzag stitch
- Overlap, bind, crimp, or otherwise finish off ends so they do not jab or poke
- When first opening a bolt of millinery wire, use care to hold the wire as you undo the little wire wrappers that hold it onto a roll; gently release the roll so that the wire expands in a controlled way, sliding around itself, otherwise, the roll will pop open and immediately become tangled

Hazard Rating: Nontoxic

Description: Solid balls are usually made of Styrofoam or rubber; hollow ones are usually made of vinyl or rubber. Available singly or in packages at craft and toy stores; inexpensive.

Application
- Good to use for large eyes or decorations
- Stack same-size Styrofoam balls for a contoured column or of a decreasing size for a tall, tapered contoured shape that could then be covered with cheesecloth and painted

Techniques and Precautions
- Use solid ball for eyeball, then slightly larger hollow ball for eyelid
- If you intend to paint or texture the surface, consider the ball's material
- Use normal safety precautions with Styrofoam

CORD—ROPE and TWINE

Hazard Rating: Nontoxic

Description: Two or more strands of fiber twisted into one. Available by the roll or ball in various sizes, fibers, and diameters from craft and hardware stores; inexpensive.

Application

- Apply to a surface for decoration
- Useful to embellish crowns and armor before applying the metallic surface
- Use to create coarse and perhaps comical hair for wigs for clowns, big puppets, and other silly characters

Techniques and Precautions

- Untwist the strands, using the fibers loose, for a different effect
- Use normal safety precautions

Hazard Rating: Use with precautions

Description: Liquid dye that is specifically made for leather will penetrate the leather skin, give it permanent color, and allow the skin to retain its flexibility. Available in bottles from craft and leather suppliers; moderate cost.

Application

- Use to permanently color a leather material
- This dye is especially effective under a metallic finish on a leather crown or small piece of armor

Techniques and Precautions

- Follow the package instructions for use
- Note safety precautions printed on the packaging

Hazard Rating: Use with precautions

Description: Round, flexible, low-density polyvinyl chloride rods. Available in various diameters (one-quarter- to four-inch), by the foot or precut length. Sold by manufacturers, suppliers of industrial packaging material, and theatrical supply stores; expensive.

Application

- Larger diameters can be sculpted into arms and legs
- Smaller diameters can be used as molding trim on walls, furniture, and millinery

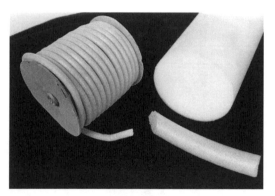

Techniques and Precautions

- Cut with serrated knife, handheld jigsaw, or band saw
- Sculpt with smaller knife or surform
- Coat with Sculpt or Coat® before painting; rod will not accept pigment without a binder or a covering of cheesecloth or muslin
- Avoid cutting with a hot knife or an electric tool that generates heat because it may generate harmful fumes
- Always use in a well-ventilated area

Hazard Rating: Nontoxic

Description: Artificial eyes for animals are usually plastic and glass or acrylic for humans. Available by the piece (plastic) or pair (glass) from craft, taxidermy, and doll making suppliers; plastic eyes are inexpensive, glass ones are moderate to expensive, depending on detail.

Application

Whenever artificial eyes are required

Techniques and Precautions

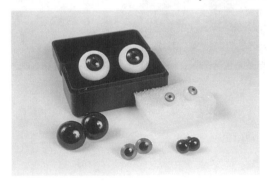

- Take care in placing the eyes so that the pupils are pointed in a direction that reflects the desired expression
  - The piece will be more believable if you carefully reproduce the tissue surrounding the eye in real life, whether it is in an animal or a human
  - Use hot glue with plastic eyes, pink wax or latex with glass eyes
  - Glass eyes tend to look more lifelike, but are fragile; plastic eyes are stronger, but tend to show surface scratches after a while
  - Use normal safety precautions

Hazard Rating: Nontoxic

Description: Outer covering of birds; name and style of feather depends on which species of bird (e.g. ostrich, turkey, coque). Supplied individually, in bunches, woven in round lengths (boas), stitched in a band, or glued onto pads. Available from leather and theatrical costume companies, hobby, and craft stores; moderate to expensive, depending on the type of feather, its coloring and preparation.

Application

Add to hats and garments for decoration

Techniques and Precautions

- To clean any type of feather, soak in soapy water, rinse, air dry, or put in clothes dryer (on air dry setting)
- Crimp to curl spine of ostrich or other plumes; use a small-diameter curling iron to curl soft parts
- Use normal safety precautions

Hazard Rating: Nontoxic

Description: Artificial flowers made of silk, fabric, or plastic. Most artificial blossoms and leaves are supplied on a wire stem, one or more per stem, one or more stems per bunch. Available from craft and hobby stores; range from inexpensive to moderate.

Application

Use as decorations on garments, millinery, or other costumes

Techniques and Precautions

- Use wire cutters to cut and use fingers or round pliers to bend stems to desired length and shape
- Can be bundled together with wire
- Sew on to hats or clothing with Silamide
- Can permanently add to an object (preferably nothing you want to wash or clean later) with hot glue
- Use normal safety precautions

Hazard Rating: Nontoxic

Description: Wheels. NOTE: Some wheels are fixed and will only move forward or backward, while others are on a spindle and will swivel all the way around. Supplied singly, or in sets of two or four from hardware stores; cost varies.

Application

Use to give an object mobility

Techniques and Precautions

- Be certain wheels are firmly installed
- Be sure you select the appropriate type of wheel mobility for your project

CHAPTER FIVE

Structure Techniques

"Where shall I begin, please, your Majesty?" he asked.

"Begin at the beginning," the King said very gravely, "and go on till you come to the end . . . then stop."

—KING OF HEARTS TO WHITE RABBIT, FROM *Alice in Wonderland* BY LEWIS CARROLL

This chapter focuses on the first step of the actual creation of your project's structure.

There are some basic tenets to be put forth here, which hold true no matter which specific technique you are applying to your project.

- Start with the inside of the project and work your way out to the surface, both when planning and constructing your project
- If the materials you have selected for your project can be sewn together, sew them rather than gluing, taping, riveting, or stapling
- If the materials you have selected for your project cannot be sewn and must be glued, use a second method of attachment as well
- Whenever possible, do not rely on glue alone—also use wire, thread, tape, monofilament, or another adhesive
- Make objects stronger by any of the following that may apply:

  use two layers

  run the grain of the layers (or the seams) perpendicular to each other

  use wire, boning, or another stiffener inside the structure

- Make objects safer and neater by finishing off the edges

The following pages identify the various structure techniques. Each technique identifies the materials and tools utilized, and lists the projects in which each technique may be found. By referring to the different project examples of each technique, the reader can begin to appreciate the slight variations and modifications that must be made to the technique each time it is applied to a new project.

The structure techniques included here are:

Shape with round reed

Shape with ethafoam

Shape with fabric

Create structure with casting latex in a negative mold

Shape with thermoplastic mesh

Shape with urethane foam

Start with found shape

SHAPE WITH ROUND REED

This material is flexible and forgiving when dry, more flexible when wet. If it is shaped when wet and held in that shape until dry, it will remain in that shape until it becomes wet again, at which point it will become flexible and bendable all over again.

The desired approach to using this material is to:

1. Determine which method you will use to hold the reed in the desired shape while it dries. There are two standard ways to do this. If the bent shape does not reach around far enough to touch itself or another piece of reed, you will need to use nails on a board on alternating sides of the bent shape, so that the piece of reed may be pressed between them and held in place by them. If the desired shapes are circular and the same piece of reed reaches all the way around to touch itself, then you can bend the reed to shape and hold it in place with a spring clip (such as a clothes-pin). Using this method, you should also tie the juncture to further secure it. Do not try to glue the joint before the reed is dry—the glue will not hold.
Note: I have tried splicing the ends of such a joint for neatness, but found that it only severely weakened the joint and therefore overlapping the ends made a much stronger piece.

2. Soak the material until it is flexible. I use a basin filled with tepid water. Loosen the ties on the reed bundle so that if you are soaking all the reed in a bolt at once, the water will saturate all sides of each piece. Soak for at least an hour—longer if the reed has a large diameter.

3. Bend to desired shape and hold it there with the method you've chosen.

4. Once dry in the desired shape, seal the reed with an acrylic medium or dilute Sculpt or Coat® so that the shape will not be lost if the piece becomes wet again. If you are not covering the shape, mix pigment in with the medium to color the reed at the same time as you seal it. This saves the time it would take to paint the object as a separate step.

SHAPE WITH ETHAFOAM

This wonderful material is lightweight, extremely strong, and—of course—relatively expensive. It is supplied in large planks that are flat and only two inches thick (they're the expensive ones), or in round, extruded rod shapes of varying diameters. Use the rod for trim and small pieces such as Nana's arms, body parts, and trim on the harp. Use the plank for larger pieces such as both cows, the elephant head, lion and tiger snouts and jaws, the eagle on the tricorne, and the tiger rug head. When working with the plank, in order to achieve a rounded shape that is thicker than two inches, glue more than one piece together and then sculpt. This material is quite expensive, so plan your pieces carefully to minimize waste. Keep only as much thickness as you need in the piece for strength; leave the rest hollow.

The desired approach to using the plank form of this material is to:

1. Plan the size and shape of each piece to get the crude form of your object.
2. Cut out each piece with either a knife, jigsaw, or band saw. I prefer handheld, nonelectrical tools, because they are safer and you have a bit more control over them. However, almost any electric tool will be faster and easier on your hands if you have a lot to cut, so judge according to your project and personal preference. There are numerous choices available in handheld knife and saw blades that you can use. I found a wavy-edged knife in a discount store a number of years ago that works very well on this material. It was quite inexpensive and hasn't ever needed to be sharpened; the waves help it to slide through the ethafoam even though the knife is no longer new.
3. Glue the pieces together, using hot, rather than cool, hot melt glue (i.e., amber rather than clear). If you are gluing small pieces, apply the melted glue evenly over the surface of one of the sides you are gluing. Press the other piece into it and hold until set—usually just a minute or two. If you are gluing large pieces, especially if you are either pulling shapes together to make a contour so there is stress on the seam or if it is particularly warm so the glue will take longer to set up, use good quality gaffer's tape to hold the ethafoam together until you are sure the glue is set.

If you are gluing large surfaces and have the equipment, use a pan in which to melt the glue and spread it onto the surface with a knife or stick to get a thin layer of the adhesive evenly spread. This process is much like applying frosting to a cake, but you must be very careful of both the pot and the heat source you use. Make sure that neither get too hot or there will be a nasty fire. We have recently found a lovely little nonstick electric frypan, which is moderately priced and much safer to use as a glue pot than a saucepan on a stove burner.

4. Use a surform or sharp knife to refine the details and contours of your piece. You will need to achieve more detail if you are not planning to cover the piece with fabric than if your finished object has a pile fabric over it. Remember, these tools have sharp edges, and they will cut through your skin just as easily as they will cut through your project, so always be wary when handling your tools.

SHAPE WITH FABRIC

This technique is almost always straight sewing as a costumer would do it. If you do not have those skills, you might want to find someone who is familiar with basic fabric cutting and stitching techniques to either help you or to do it for you. Even if you do find a talented, willing, and skilled helper, the chapters in pattern development and costume construction in *The Costume Designer's Handbook*, by Rosemary Ingham and Liz Covey (Heinemann, 1992), will give you an excellent framework for your patterning and sewing activities.

The desired approach is to:

1. Plan (pattern) the shape of the pieces. This is done either by drawing out a flat pattern or by draping the shape on an existing three-dimensional object. This can be a dress form or your sculpted object. The elephant body was simply a rectangle of fabric that spanned the distance between the front skier and the rear one. Nana's body was cut from an oversized one-piece animal body pattern we have in the shop. The tiger rug body was a stylized version of an animal skin cut up the belly and flattened out on the floor. The aging stripper costume was a parody of the real chorus costumes worn by the other dancers. Clearly there are as many variations as there are projects.

2. Cut the pieces, allowing for ease, seams, padding, and the like. At this point, you should know how many layers and what kind of fabric you are going to be cutting and whether any of them will vary in size from your pattern pieces. The *Midsummer* crowns were two layers of stiff stuff and a top layer of the sparkly costume fabric, all cut the same size and stitched together as though they were a single piece. The robe of the Ghost of Christmas Future was cut as two garments. The under robe was cut of black cotton and only full enough to permit the movement needed; the upper robe was cut of black tissue lamé to give it a mysterious sheen and cut much fuller, so that it would move and flow in a very dramatic way.

3. Sew the pieces together either by hand or machine, depending on the project. Your choice of material and availability of various machines will dictate the type of sewing machine you use. The aging stripper bean bags

were made of Lycra so they would stretch and move, and were stitched with an overlock sewing machine to give a strong but stretchy seam that would give with the fabric. If we had had a sewing machine made specifically for sewing leather, the elf shoes might have been a bit easier. We didn't, but chose our most powerful industrial machine with a good leather needle in it and it worked just fine.

CREATE STRUCTURE WITH CASTING LATEX

We start this technique with an existing negative mold that we will use to create a positive latex piece—a method called "slush" casting.

1. The mold needs to be clean, dry, and in good repair.
2. Prepare the latex. For large pieces, we use casting latex, which is less pure and less expensive than the latex you would get in a one- or eight-ounce bottle at a theatrical makeup store. Decide how firm you want the finished piece to be to determine whether or not you will need to add a filler. Both the latex and the filler are available from some theatrical makeup and craft supply houses. By not adding filler to our latex armor and Cowardly Lion, the pieces remained flexible. We did, however, add pigment so we'd have a base coat of color built in, which saved a step. Our armor pieces were all colored black as a base, so that when we added silver over it there was really good depth to the sculpted parts. We added a flesh tint to the lion mask so that it would match the face of the wearer and the lion makeup could then be applied over the lion face as though it was a single piece.

   A good rule of thumb for starting to mix a Caucasian flesh tone is one part red to two parts yellow. Adding a green or brown pigment will give a more ethnic tone. Remember that when you are tinting liquid latex, the latex dries many times darker than in its liquid state. When you are doing a Caucasian tint, it is better to err on the side of too pale than too dark. Start with very little and test it. You can always add more color if there is not enough. Adding too much color becomes wasteful if you have to start thinning your batch down.
3. Pour the prepared latex into the negative mold up to where you want your finished piece to be (usually this is to the top of the mold).
4. Let the latex set until there is a layer of the desired thickness from the mold inward. Latex cures from the plaster toward the center of a negative mold. You will need to gain a little firsthand experience with this to judge how thick you want a particular piece, but it won't take long for you to get the feel of this technique.

CREATE STRUCTURE
WITH CASTING LATEX

5. When you think your piece is ready, drain all of the liquid latex that remains in the center of the mold back into the container. If you don't, the remainder will slide down to the bottom and puddle there. It will eventually cure and, depending on how much there was, may make the area at the bottom of the mold noticeably thicker and more rigid than the rest of the piece. You can use this to your advantage if there is a part of the cast piece that you want to make thicker than the rest.

6. When the inside surface of the latex is completely cured it will feel dry to the touch. You should be able to press on it and not leave a fingerprint. Dust this surface with talc and remove any excess. If you do not use the talc, when two parts of this surface come in contact they will stick together. Once you have dusted with the talc, you will never have to do it again, but it is necessary this first time.

7. Once the inside of your molded piece is powdered and cleaned off, it is time to remove it from the mold. Place your thumb any place where the latex meets the plaster, and peel the latex inward away from the plaster until you can grasp it. Then gently pull more and more of it away from the mold until it is completely out. I always think this is a very exciting moment, especially if it is the first piece pulled from a particular mold; it's even more exciting if you created the mold yourself!

8. Clean off the outside of the latex piece with a damp cloth, trim any excess from the edges with scissors, and admire your work!

SHAPE WITH THERMOPLASTIC MESH

This material is surprisingly easy to work with. There is little to no waste and you can change the piece any time you want to by heating the material and reshaping it. This characteristic is also the primary drawback, as it will lose its shape whenever it gets too warm, whether you want it to or not!

1. Create your pattern pieces in paper, then transfer these shapes to the mesh.
2. Cut the mesh into pieces of the desired shape and size.
3. Using a hair dryer or warm water bath in a shallow pan over a burner, heat the pieces of mesh and bend into the desired shape.
4. The mesh will bond strongly to itself when heated. No other adhesive is required.
5. If you are draping the mesh over a positive mold, you should press aluminum foil over the mold shape as a release before applying the mesh so it will not stick to the mold.
6. Edges of the mesh may be folded over themselves to create a smoother and slightly stronger edge. Darts may be created by folding the mesh over on itself for extreme shaping and the mesh can just be pulled to make a piece a little wider or narrower in a particular area.
7. Once the desired shape is achieved, let the piece cool and dry thoroughly.
8. Color the piece with pigment or bronzing powder in medium. Attach found objects for decoration, using medium-temperature hot glue.

SHAPE WITH URETHANE FOAM

The only really tricky part to working with urethane foam, or any material that has an appreciable thickness, is to allow for the difference between the inside and the outside dimension when you are cutting the pieces. For example, the Radio Man and the shampoo bottle had to fit a person inside them. The Radio Man could be cut pretty exactly since it was a rectangle and the outside dimensions would be the same as the inside plus the thickness of the foam. The shampoo bottle, however, was round and the inside dimension lost about two inches from the outside measurement in a distance of about three feet. Being aware of this phenomenon will save having to recut and add a piece in.

1. Pattern your pieces. You may want to cut actual paper pieces if you need to drape them together and fine-tune the shape with something irregular like the rooster. Or you may only need to determine what the dimensions of each piece need to be, if you are cutting something geometric like the Radio Man.
2. Cut the foam. If you have a sharp band, jig-, table saw, or an electric knife and you like using power tools, fine. I don't, and prefer to use a good pair of large scissors—either will work.
3. If you are making an irregular shape and want to test the pieces now that they are cut, you can pin them together using strong, long t-pins (see picture on p. 31). When you have corrected the shapes to your satisfaction, it is time to glue.
4. Apply the adhesive to both edges of the pieces that are going together. Follow package directions carefully, especially in regards to the amount of ventilation you need in your work area and the length of time you should wait after applying the adhesive before you place the two edges together. Most foam adhesives work like a contact cement and need to be either tacky or dry before the edges touch each other to ensure a good bond. Be sure to leave areas of seams open if there is to be rigging installed or other internal work that can't be done until the piece is at least partially together.

START WITH FOUND SHAPE

There are some projects, or parts of some projects, which just lend themselves to utilizing a part or piece that already exists. When we found an already made stuffed hen, for example, which we could mount on an already manufactured, battery-operated car chassis, we were delighted! Likewise with the felt hat forms for the ostrich warbonnets and a ready-made animal head for our Nana. I intentionally went on a search for the perfect strong, lightweight helmet shape for our skiing lion and tiger and was thrilled to find my solution in our local Army-Navy store!

Using found objects isn't lazy or shameful: I believe it's just as creative as building an object from scratch. The trick, if there is any, lies in being thoroughly honest about whether or not what you have found really fits your criteria and can be successfully modified to create your project.

Detail Techniques

"The time has come," the Walrus said,
"To talk of many things:
Of shoes—and ships—and sealing wax—
Of cabbages—and kings—
And why the sea is boiling hot—
And whether pigs have wings."

—"THE WALRUS AND THE CARPENTER"
FROM *Through the Looking Glass* BY LEWIS CARROLL

The details of a project are those additions that give the piece its definition, both in terms of appearance and function. The talking tiger rug must have animal eyes; the *Gypsy* cow's eyes should be able to close in a wink, or blink and reopen; the rooster has to turn its head from side-to-side and flap its wings.

The detail techniques included in this chapter are:

Pad shape

Place flex screen

Rig moving parts

Apply stiffener

Sculpt detail

Apply connectors

Once the framework or skeleton of a shape is formed, it may need some padding to give it the appropriate dimension or thickness, just as our body skeleton doesn't look right without muscle, other internal "padding," and skin. Each of the examples here utilizes a slightly different method, but the end result is a rounder, more padded shape.

Our rooster's wings were made of a layer of foam on the bottom and polyfill on top so that the suggestion of feathers could be stitched into them to give added dimension and detail.

We used dried peas for the breast padding in the aging stripper costume because of their weight and the way they would move. They were encased in "breast bags" of a double layer of Lycra so they would be a bit bouncy.

Additional dimension was added to the contours of the harp by gluing one-half-inch round lengths of ethafoam rod to the plywood shape. This material gave a rounded, carved look to the harp without adding any extra weight, since the three-quarter-inch plywood frame was already heavy enough.

We wanted a rather skeletal effect for the Ghost of Christmas Future, but did put extra-large shoulder pads on the top of the backpack frame at the "shoulders" so that the robes would fall out away from the body of the person inside.

PLACE FLEX SCREEN

Placing screening in an opening in a costume piece will permit the person inside to see out, will allow a flow of air for breathing, and will prevent others from seeing inside the costume easily.

1. Planning the placement of the screening is foremost. Two areas of vision, one at eye level of the wearer and another below that, will accomplish two objectives. If this is a walkabout costume, the person inside will be able to see ahead through the upper area of screening as well as see down to the ground to find steps, curbs, or other obstructions through the lower screen. Air will circulate more freely inside the costume with two areas of screening, especially if the wearer breathes in through the nose and out through the mouth, or vice versa. The lion and tiger had only one screen each, but they were large (the animals' mouths were open in fierce, growling poses) and the lower edge of the neck fur was full and fell away from the body enough so that fresh air could pass through. There was only one screen in the under robe of the Ghost of Christmas Future, as the wearer could see down from inside the robes easily and because the outer layer of robe was sheer enough to see through without a screen. This made the costume more magical because even the screening was concealed.
2. Cut the screening about three-quarters of an inch larger than the opening it conceals.
3. Bind the edge all around with twill tape or seam binding, or with a fabric that is heavy enough to protect the eyes and skin of the person wearing the costume from the ends of the fibers of the screening.
4. Place the screen on the inside of the costume piece and hot glue it in place.
5. Paint details on the screening if needed, such as eyes or a tongue.

This is where the technique of puppeteering and just plain ingenuity come into their own. I do some of my best problem solving during my morning walk. Rigging moving parts is usually the knottiest of problems to unravel; working this part out can take a walk and a half to solve. Several of the project examples here fall into the grouping which I call "pulling a piece away from its original position and having it automatically return to that position"; the *Gypsy* cow's eyelids and mouth, the Milky White cow's mouth, the tiger rug's ears, and the rooster's wings. Each of them pull away by the same mechanism: a concealed cord with a ring on the end of it. Three of them (the cows' mouths and the tiger rug's ears) have the cords pass through tubing to provide free passage through a solid piece of material. The return to the original position is a little more varied. Both cows' mouths and the tiger's ears are spring-loaded to return automatically. The *Gypsy* cow's eyelids are weighted in the back to open when released from the pulled-shut position and the rooster's wings pull down by cords to flap and return to a normal position by gravity.

We wanted the rooster's head to be able to turn from side-to-side so we used a dowel inside a tube (CPVC pipe) to accomplish this. The tubing was inserted into the rooster from the bottom opening and was securely hot glued to the inside of the lower neck. The dowel, which was longer than the tube, was placed through the tube to the top of the rooster's head (one seam of which had not been glued closed) and firmly hot glued to the inside of the rooster's head. The bottom end of the dowel was about six inches longer than the end of the tube, and both were long enough that the hands of the puppeteer would not be seen holding and manipulating them. The head movement was then easily manipulated by holding the tube still and twisting the dowel inside it.

The open-and-close movement of the talking tiger's lower jaw is completely controlled by the hand of the actor inside the head. The fingers of the hand fit between two parallel quarter-inch dowels and the thumb in the lower jaw fits into a leather loop attached to a similar single dowel in the lower jaw.

The distance the tiger rug's jaw opened had to be limited to a realistic amount. This was done by extending both upper and lower parts behind the pivot point of the jaw and cutting out a V-shaped wedge so that as the jaw part in front of the pivot point was lowered, it would be stopped when the V was closed behind the pivot point in the back. The pivot point was connected by a folded piece of leather both front and back to allow free movement in the simplest way.

Diagrams of all these mechanisms appear in the project section of this book.

Stiffeners help to establish the form, shape, or structure of a piece. Stiffeners are not necessarily rigid—often they are just stiffer than the materials they are used with.

A range of stiffeners is used in the various projects, beginning with the softest, which is the inherently stiff fabric known as "stiff stuff." We used that in the base that goes around the wheels of the hen to mask them, and in all three crowns.

Many layers of the plastic cream known as Sculpt or Coat® was applied to very brittle Styrofoam boaters to stiffen and strengthen them when they were modified to be used as tambourine hats for *Will Rogers Follies*.

Steel hoop boning was used in the wings of the rooster. The majority of the piece of boning stiffens the inside of the wing. A pull cord attaches to the protruding end of the boning and is inserted into the body of the rooster at the point of natural attachment of wing to body. When the cords of each wing were pulled, they lifted the wings to make a flapping motion.

The same boning pieces were used on the *Mikado* head-piece to protrude so that tassels could be suspended from the ends of them. Popsicle sticks would have worked as well in both instances.

Heavy-duty stiffeners in the form of lengths of CPVC pipe were used to extend and join the uprights of the backpack frame that was the base structure of the Ghost of Christmas Future. Others joined together to form upper and lower arms on the same piece.

SCULPT DETAIL

There are two ways to achieve detail and contours: either put more of a material on to the piece (additive), or take some of the piece away (subtractive). Often the subtractive method requires a little more care, because if too much material is cut away, it is seldom satisfactory and sometimes not even possible to replace. The body parts project is our example of subtractive detailing and simply involves cutting or scraping away enough of the ethafoam rod to create the details of hands and feet that make these pieces of plastic look like body parts.

The details on our peg leg—the large splinters that become apparent after Pegleg has a second encounter with the whale—are made of the same materials as the original piece to indicate that the splinters were once part of the original whole peg leg. The wrinkles and contours on the Salieri mask are made of the same material, the plaster bandage, but are painted later to highlight them as grotesqueries.

The remainder of our project examples utilize materials which are added to and are different from the primary material of the piece. This helps to set them apart and make them more noticeable as details. The nose, teeth, and eye sockets of the lion, tiger, and tiger rug are sculpted of Friendly plastic. The eagle tricorne's feet and the asp on the Egyptian headpiece are sculpted of air-drying clay.

The variety of objects available for connecting is limited only by your imagination. A few of our favorites are included here.

The elephant on skis (two people, one in front, one behind) had to come apart and pack in luggage to go on an airplane. We also wanted it to come apart relatively easily if something should happen to either skier during performance, so we chose hook-and-pad tape since it fit all our criteria. We also used it on the straps on the elf shoes, since there was not much stress or pull on them. It was useful to have a little freedom to adjust them, and the tape could be sewn in the inside where it would not show.

The flowers on the Will's sister costumes had to stay on until they were removed for washing and did not have any stress on them when in place, so our connectors of choice for these circumstances were snaps.

We needed to join the upper and lower arm pieces of the Ghost of Christmas Future and attach them to the shoulders of this spectre. A loose, flexible connection was needed. It had to allow freedom of movement, but not come undone under any circumstances. We chose quick links. They are easily installed into the ends of the conduit by drilling two opposing holes just in from the end of the conduit, fitting a quick link inside the conduit past the holes, then placing a strong wire through the holes and securing it in place to hold the end of the link inside the pipe. Repeat this with the end of the other pipe and join the two together with a third quick link. You can do this with just the two links, one in each pipe end, but you won't have quite as much freedom of movement without the third.

CHAPTER SEVEN

Surface Techniques

"If it was so, it might be;
and if it were so, it would be;
but as it isn't, it ain't. That's logic."

—TWEEDLEDEE,
FROM *Through the Looking Glass* BY LEWIS CARROLL

Now that you have created the structure of your project and added the details to make it look like and do what it should, it is time to decorate the outside surface to give your project that final perfect look; to fine-tune the object for surface texture, color, and detail so there will be no mistaking what this object is and does. Although there are many choices and you are limited only by your own resourcefulness, they all fall into a few basic groups. Select one or use a combination of several in the same project.

The techniques are:

Cover the surface with fabric

Paint color with texture on the surface

Create dimension using color

Soft sculpt details

Add found object details

You can use almost any kind of fabric as a covering, although some lend themselves to this more readily than others. There are several good rules of thumb to follow in narrowing down your choices.

1. Choose a fabric that will communicate the reality of the surface you want to suggest. Fake fur in almost any animal pattern is readily available for creatures like the lion, both tigers, the cow for *Gypsy*, the hen (even though hens have feathers, not fur), Nana, even the "ermine" trim on the crown for *Me and My Girl*. The elephant had to communicate the relatively hairless but very wrinkly texture of an elephant's hide. Cotton Lycra was the fabric of choice for the shampoo bottle to give a smooth, matte surface like a plastic bottle. The Ghost of Christmas Future was designed to be mysterious and magical and we wanted it to be visible in low, intermittent light on stage. Tissue lamé was a logical choice since it is very lightweight, moves well, and is moderately reflective so the folds would catch the light in an otherworldly way. Stretch terry cloth was the ideal choice for the rooster because it has a little surface texture and has sufficient two-way stretch to accommodate the contours with a minimum of seams. The fabric on the harp was gauze, which was applied for function rather than decoration as it provided a surface of even and subtle texture to make the transition from foam to plywood nearly invisible. We applied the fabric with diluted white glue, which allowed us to paint the surface of both materials with bronzing powder in medium.
2. The more rounded your sculpted shape, the more stretchy you want the fabric covering to be. Vellux, which holds its shape, is fine for the flat and geometric Radio Man, whereas a very giving, two-way stretch terry cloth is the fabric of choice for the rooster.
3. Attach the fabric to the sculpted shape in each place the shape changes contours, either by going in (an undercut) or out.
4. The more textured the fabric, the less the detail on the understructure will show. For example, you can save time on the under surfaces of pieces like the lion and tiger if you cover them with a thick-pile fake fur fabric.

5. Use an appropriate material to attach the fabric to the understructure. Often this will be an adhesive, but remember that it is better to sew pieces together whenever possible. Where there are openings in a costume through which the wearer will put a body part, such as the shampoo bottle, I prefer to sew the fabric to the inside around the arm, neck, and face holes. If you use an adhesive, it is likely that some of it will extend beyond the fabric on the inside and remain gummy and gooey where the wearer will touch it.

6. Fabric can make an ordinary piece look like something special. We wanted the eagle tricorne to be shiny and a particular shade of royal blue. The most economical way to do this was to take a basic black one and cover it with a highly reflective, royal blue lamé. Covering the surface of a hat is not very different from covering any other three-dimensional object.

PAINT COLOR WITH TEXTURE ON THE SURFACE

Often a single color on an object is sufficient to convey what that object is: brown for the ass head; white for Milky White and Pegleg; gold for the asp on the Egyptian headpiece, the eagle on the tricorne, and the balls on the crown for *Me and My Girl*.

Facial features may be effectively communicated as a single color. For example, pink for cheeks on the elephant and black on the noses, eye rims, and gums of the lion and tigers. This is especially true for critters that do not have human features, like pink cheeks, which gives a cartoonlike quality to their faces.

Stenciling a repeating design on the fabric of the Red Death costume and painting on bronzing powder in medium freehand was a very minimalist approach. Yet it was visually effective from the audience.

Painting with pigment in a polymer medium is extremely useful. It lets the craftsperson select the least expensive yet adequate pigment (casein) and mix it with an acrylic polymer medium. This binder lets the pigment stick to nonporous surfaces. (With porous surfaces, like cotton or wood, pigments can soak in by themselves, but with nonporous surfaces you need a binder that'll help the pigment stick to the surface.) The binder will also make the surface more water repellent and a little stiff, if the material is flexible to begin with. Depending on the type of binder you choose, you can have a flat or glossy surface. The proportion of pigment to binder can also be adjusted and varied for the intensity of color desired. Texture (such as sand, cornmeal, oatmeal, or other grainy material) may be added to the medium.

CREATE DIMENSION USING COLOR

This is the technique artists use when painting on canvas or other flat surfaces. According to Webster's II New Riverside dictionary, *chiaroscuro* is the technique of using light and shade in a pictorial representation, and numerous art texts detail the reasons why the eye can be fooled by the careful use of light and dark. There are many excellent discussions of dimension and color theory; Corson and Corey each discuss warm and cool colors, light and shadow in their books (see the bibliography).

Makeup is a classic example of applying color to a three-dimensional surface to create dimension. In its simplest form, the color of makeup emphasizes desirable features such as eyes, cheeks, and lips, and minimizes unwanted characteristics like a crooked nose, bags under the eyes, and multiple chins. A more extreme application of this technique exists for the stage, where often the contours of the actor's face must be changed to better convey the character being portrayed. When those usually undesirable characteristics of crooked nose, eye bags, or wrinkly, scarred, or disfigured skin are exactly what the actor needs, the makeup artist often creates the desired dimension and contour with color alone.

The intent of this book is to demystify three-dimensional projects. Most of the principles and techniques are simple, yet I am always surprised and delighted when my eye is fooled and perceives contours and shapes where there are none. This, to me, is real magic!

Here is the dimension-with-color story simplified:

light=out

dark=in

reds and yellows (brighter)=out

blues and greens (darker)=in

(Black and white are not considered "colors" and therefore suggest the extremes of presence or absence of a material.) There, that's it! All the rest is art and illusion!

Test this notion by taking a black makeup pencil and drawing a line along the edge of one of your eyelids right next to the lashes. Stand a little distance from a mirror and stare straight into it. The eye with the black liner will look noticeably larger than the other one.

CREATE DIMENSION USING COLOR

Here's how it translates for projects:

Paint the entire surface of a slightly dimensional object black or a very dark color. Overbrush the raised surfaces with a bright color, such as a metallic bronzing powder. The raised surfaces will appear many times more raised than if the whole surface were the same bright color. See the chain mail, latex armor, Salieri mask, and harp projects for examples of this technique.

To make a surface appear much more rounded, as if to pop up toward you, paint a darker shade around the outside and a lighter shade toward the center of a flat, or slightly rounded, surface. See the roster project as an example of this aspect.

Push black (or a dark color) into the crevice of two surfaces of different height. The crevice will become much deeper and the piece may look older and more real. Using the eyeliner example, take a brush and blend the top edge of the black line upward onto the lid so that the darkest black is along the lash edge. As the color fades to gray, then to the tone of the lid, not only will the eye look larger, the lid will look more interesting because it now has more depth and dimension. The elf shoe project is a good example.

Create depth and dimension by using a darker color behind a lighter one. This technique lends itself to materials such as fringe, and soft feathers such as ostrich, where a darker shade of the same fringe is placed behind a lighter one, or a darker plume is attached to the back of the spine of a lighter one to give added depth, dimension, and interest. See the ostrich warbonnet for our project example of this technique.

SOFT SCULPT DETAILS

Some details, especially on a figure that is more cartoonlike than realistic, are most effective if soft sculpted by cutting a slightly enlarged shape out of the appropriate fabric, sewing one edge onto the piece, stuffing the underneath with something such as polyfill, and then sewing the other edge down. An example from our projects is the comb and wattles on the rooster.

ADD FOUND OBJECT DETAILS

Found objects can provide the widest variety of decorations for your project and are probably the most traditional way of adding finishing touches. Artificial flowers, Styrofoam balls, bells, bows, fringe, tassels, mirrors, sequins, and silly paper cord are among just a few.

This is where they are used in our projects:

artificial flowers: ass head, *Gypsy* cow

Styrofoam balls: *Me and My Girl* crown

bells: Milky White cow

bows: Milky White cow, *Gypsy* cow

fringe: aging stripper

tassels: aging stripper, *Mikado* headpiece

mirrors: ostrich warbonnet

sequins: aging stripper, *Midsummer* crowns

silly paper cord: harp

Use whatever means of attachment that is most appropriate: sewing, hot glue, or wire. Remember, if you are going to need to clean either the object or the decoration, the decoration should be attached in a way that permits easy removal and replacement. The snaps on the flowers of the costumes for Will's sisters is one example.

Projects

Actor Was "Miscast"

Paul Fifield, who is studying acting in Cambridge, England, agreed to help his friend and fellow student, Kate Freeland, by letting her cast his nude body in plaster so she could make a statue of a Greek god for her garden.

But Kate was new at sculpting and used hard-setting wall plaster instead of the no-stick kind.

Doctors had to chip him out of the cast, and removed much of his body hair in the "extremely painful" process. Said Fifield, 19: "Kate was reading a book on how to do it but I don't think she had got further than the preface."

—*Boston Globe*, April 23, 1995

The projects really need no further introduction. They are presented in the following groups for ease of comparison:

- Animals
- Costume garments
- Accessories
- Objects
- Prosthetics

You can find the projects listed by name (ass head, elf shoes, and so forth) within each group, starting on page 179, along with the tools, materials, and techniques used.

ASS HEAD

The director of this production of A Midsummer Night's Dream asked for a larger-than-life ass head that was open enough for the actor's head and face to show through and his voice to be easily heard. We feel strongly that, whenever possible, the weight of an object placed over a person's head should be located on the shoulders rather than on the head and spine. This will prevent any possibility of headache, nausea, or other symptoms that can result from excess pressure on the neck and spinal column.

Appearance Goals

- This is one of Shakespeare's fanciful comedies, so there needs to be a feeling of fun and fantasy about this head that will capture the spirit of the comedy

- Needs a see-through head so actor can be seen and heard
- Should have a lock of hair between the ears, and some flowers

Function Goals

- Has to be lightweight and balanced so the actor has mobility without the head falling off
- Eyes should also be lightweight and not obstruct the actor's field of vision

Tools

Cutting pliers
Glue gun
Clothespins

Materials

Round reed
Fabric for ears
Ribbons and flowers
Pigment in medium
Urethane foam

Structure Techniques

Sculpt shape with round reed

Detail Techniques

Sculpt details: Pieces of urethane foam lightly painted can sugest eyes and nostrils.

Surface Techniques

- Paint with pigment in medium
- Add found object details: Flowers, front forelock, and mane

The cow costume in the musical, *Gypsy*, appears fairly early on in the story, and is really included to drive home the point that Mama Rose would always give the best roles to her daughter June (the front of the cow) and the supporting roles to her other daughter Louise (the rear end of the cow). This is musical comedy, and we couldn't resist the temptation to add a wreath of flowers to the cow head and a bow to her neck.

Appearance Goals

The costume should look somewhat homemade

Function Goals

- It has to be a two-person cow so that the audience can see Louise in the rear half
- Mouth has to open wide enough so that audience can see June in the head
- Eyelids should blink

Tools

Serrated knife
Surform
Glue gun

Materials

Ethafoam plank
Pile fabric
Balls—solid and hollow
Tubing (straws)
Springs
Weights
Cord

Structure Techniques

Sculpt shape with ethafoam plank

Detail Techniques

Rig moving parts: In this case, the eyes and the mouth

For the eyes:
- Cut a hollow ball slightly larger than the solid balls used for the eyeballs in half (use one half for each eye)
- Reinforce the edges with millinery wire
- Place each half around a solid ball
- Use a straight piece of coat-hanger wire to form the pivot point for the eyelid to turn around the eyeball

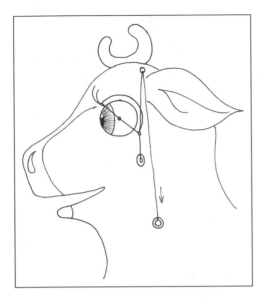

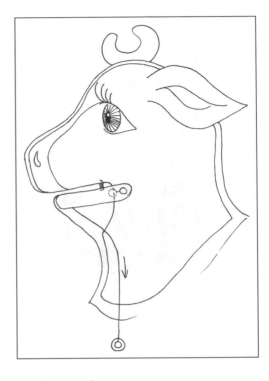

- Attach a washer to one end of a rigging cord as a weight
- Attach the cord to the back of the eyelid by both tying and gluing it so that the weight hangs down a couple of inches
- Thread the cord through a smooth loop at the top of the inside of the head
- Leave enough length to manipulate the eye wink below the neck of the head
- Attach a ring for ease in finding and winking the eye
- Repeat if you want both eyes to wink

For the mouth:
- Attach the back of each side of the lower jaw to the upper with a strip of fabric for stability
- Imbed springs to hold lower jaw closed and secure with hot glue
- Install one end of pull cord in front of jaw
- Add pull ring to other end

Surface Techniques

- Cover surface with fabric: Use the same fur fabric used for the body
- Paint surface of the eyes with pigment in medium
- Add found object details: Flowers on head, bow on neck, eyelashes on eyelids

MILKY WHITE COW

from Into the Woods

The technical aspects of *Into the Woods* are extensive and varied. In the story, Milky White is supposed to be able to eat certain ingredients identified by the Witch and produce a magic potion when she's milked that will cure the spell cast on the Baker and his Wife. Because the production was presented in the round, we had no other option than to make her hollow and large enough to hold all the props inside. This consideration dictated the rest of her structure in terms of size, strength, and how she was dismantled.

Appearance Goals

A white fairy tale cow that matches the description in the script

Function Goals

- Has to roll onstage on its own wheels
- Has to hold numerous objects, including a shoe, hair, a cape, and a golden egg

Note: Because our Milky White was created for a production that was completely in the round, nothing could be masked by the "upstage" side of this cow.

Tools

Pliers
Serrated knife
Glue gun
Surform

Materials

Copper pipe
CPVC pipe
Ethafoam plank
Nylon rope
Springs
Wheels
Plaster bandage
Pigment in medium

Structure Techniques

- Assemble CPVC frame
- Sculpt shape with ethafoam plank

Detail Techniques

Rig moving parts:
- Mouth: Install lower jaw on springs, which will hold it closed unless manually opened by an actor
- Wheels: Fit into sleeves that hold them into the bottom end of each CPVC pipe inner leg

Surface Techniques

- Coat surface with plaster bandage
- Paint surface of eyes with pigment in medium
- Add found object details: Nylon rope that's been unraveled for tail and "hair"

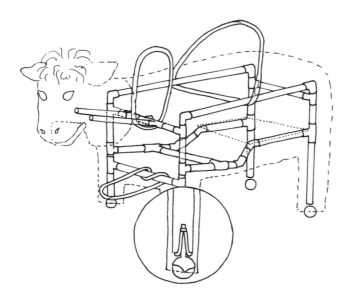

We do costumes for a group of Olympic-quality skiers who entertain at ski competitions. The skiers are classified as either "jumpers" or "ballet" skiers, and have quite a set of requirements for their costumes. The first requirement is "It's gotta show on snow," so white and very pale colors are out. We developed a basic set of patterns that we use for all the garments, which pull on over ski books, fit over ski parkas, do not fall off, or obscure vision when a skier turns upside down as they often do, and so forth. The other necessity is every costume must fold up and fit into regular airplane luggage, because most of their performances are in Europe and Japan. The elephant, for example, which had to costume two skiers and break away safely in the event one of them fell, still had to pack flat and small. The end result was pretty silly and was featured on sportscasts in Japan.

Appearance Goals

- Needs to look like a circus elephant on skis from a distance
- How many toes does a real elephant have?? That depends on where it is from—either 3 or 4 on each foot. This one became the designer's choice, but at least we checked and that's important

Function Goals

- Needs to be lightweight and have enough visibility so that two professional skiers can ski downhill in this costume. Legs get made as pants that pull on with suspenders to hold them up
- Body gets made as a blanket so that the skier in back can see down and out as far as possible
- A view screen is essential for the skier in front

- Has to break down to fit in luggage to transport to a performance abroad

- Schedule fittings for height of lift poles, length, and width of blanket, and for location of view screen for the skier in front

Tools

Glue gun
Sewing machine

Materials

Ethafoam plank for structure of head and rear support
CPVC pipe for lightweight lift poles
Gray felt for body, legs, face, and ears
Pink pile fabric for ear and trunk lining
Pink felt for toenails
Solid balls for eyes
Flex screen
Velcro
Acetate taffeta and sequins to decorate blanket
Ethafoam rod with 3" diameter for trunk
Spray adhesive
Steel boning

Structure Techniques

- Sculpt shape with ethafoam plank of head and rear support
- Shape garment with fabric: Body and legs will be made of muslin; two pairs of baggy pants will have straight legs

Detail Techniques

- Add facial details: Eyes and trunk. Drape felt on the eyelids as they don't have to move

- Apply connectors: Use Velcro for easy breakdown

Surface Techniques

- Cover surface with fabric: Body and legs will be made of felt (see below for technique of felt on legs and trunk)

    Cover muslin legs to inseam with grey felt made into tubes twice as long as legs

    Sew at top edge onto muslin leg at inseam level

    Scrunch felt leg onto muslin leg, so felt looks like wrinkly, saggy skin of an elephant; use the same technique on ethafoam rod trunk, so felt trunk skin looks wrinkly

    Machine sew sequins on blanket

- Paint color and texture on the surface of the eyes
- Add found object details: Add bows on forehead and tail

Although this animal is a minor character in *Into the Woods*, it needs to be able to make an entrance onstage by itself, with no visible means of propulsion. It also has to produce a golden egg—thank goodness for panty hose!

Appearance Goals

Built for the musical *Into the Woods*, it has to look like a fairy-tale hen

Function Goals

- It has to be self-propelled to make its own entrance onstage
- It has to produce a golden egg

Tools

Zigzag sewing machine
Cutting pliers

Materials

Ready-made plush, stuffed hen rod puppet, with a hollow pocket that contains the rod to puppeteer her head (what a find!)
Radio-controlled toy car
Silamide
Stiff stuff
Millinery wire
Stretchy fabric
Pile fabric

Structure Techniques

Start with found shape: Remove exterior coating of car, i.e., the plastic body; remove rod from inside hen

Detail Techniques

- Apply stiffener by making a band of two layers of stiff stuff wide enough to measure the height of the car wheels plus a little, and long enough to reach around outside of all four wheels of the car body

- Add another stiffener by applying millinery wire to both long edges of band. Bend it loosely enough around the outside edge of wheels of car base so that all wheels turn freely, and stitch closed. It now becomes a border around the car base, concealing the wheels
- Cut a piece of green stretch fabric to fit across the top surface of the border
- Cut a hole in the stretch fabric to let the radio antenna stand up
- Sew stretch fabric to inside of top edge of border. Border will now lift on and off the car body, allowing the antenna to keep its upright position
- Hand sew hen to stretch fabric so that the antenna will fit up inside neck of hen and remote control will work

Surface Techniques

Cover the surface with green pile fabric so that the wheels are concealed and the hen will appear to be sitting in a grass nest

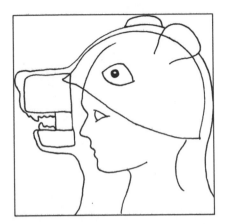

The lion and tiger were other characters from the ski show, and had to be realistic- (and fierce-!) looking. The costumes also had to stay on when the skier was upside down and be easily changed into, in addition to the other stipulations mentioned. Although normally we don't like to mount a full head on the head of the wearer (see ass head project), the weight in these two head was quite small and was offset by the quite strong basic structure of the helmet liner.

Appearance Goals

- One-person animal costume to be worn by a "jumping" skier
- Has to look like a fierce circus animal

Function Goals

- Costume has to allow full mobility of skier
- Has to be a quick change both in and out by a skier who has gloves on
- The animal head has to allow visibility and to stay on, even when the skier is upside down performing a fancy jump

Tools

Glue gun
Serrated knife
Surform
Orangewood stick

Materials

Helmet liner for structure of head
Plastic animal eyes
Ethafoam plank for snout and jaw shaping
Pile fabric for surface covering
Flex screen
Friendly plastic
Pigment in medium

Structure Techniques

- Start with found shape: In this case, the helmet provides a structure for the animal head
- Sculpt shape of snout and lower jaw with ethafoam plank

SKIING LION AND TIGER

ANIMALS

Detail Techniques

- Add facial details: Apply ears, eyes, and jaw structure to helmet
- Sculpt detail of teeth and nose with Friendly plastic
- Place flex screen and chin elastic

Surface Techniques

- Cover surface with pile fabric
- Paint surface of eye sockets, nose, and teeth with pigment in polymer medium (see Surface Techniques—Paint color with texture on the surface)

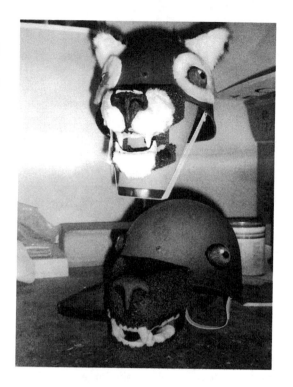

NANA

from Peter Pan

For a long time I have been concerned about the basic difference between the anatomy of a dog and the anatomy of a person playing a dog, and how to reconcile the two. Most parade heads large enough to fit over the head of the person wearing it have the opening in the bottom, where the human neck is, which is fine if the person wearing the head is going to be standing up like a human. If the person is going to be on all fours like a dog, the person's head must enter the parade head from the back, otherwise the face of the head will be facing the floor, not looking out at the audience. The length of the forearms is a problem of proportion, and is best solved with arm extenders for the human.

Appearance Goals

Built for the musical *Peter Pan*, this costume should resemble an Old English sheepdog. Beware: Old English sheepdogs do not have tails!

Function Goals

- The person wearing it should be on all fours and so arms (front legs) should have extenders on them to make human arms proportionally as long as dog arms, for sitting and crawling around like a dog
- The opening of the parade head should be at the back of the head rather than at the bottom

Tools

Serrated knife
Glue gun

Materials

Preformed celastic dog head
Ethafoam rod for arm extenders
Pile fabric for surface covering
Flex screen
Spray adhesive

Structure Techniques

- Start with found shape: Cut the head hole in back of uncovered animal head

- Shape arm extenders with ethafoam rod (with 3″ diameter)
- Shape body with pile fabric and make arms long enough to accommodate extensions

Detail Techniques

Place flex screen in eye and mouth areas

Surface Techniques

Cover surface with pile fabric

This rooster appeared in a children's musical with several other animal rod puppets. The rooster had to be able to turn its head from side-to-side and flap its wings, and be operated by a five- or six-year-old child. Not only did we have to figure out the mechanisms for the required movements, but they also had to be simple and strong enough so a young child could operate them successfully.

Appearance Goals

This rooster had to look like Tomie de Paola's rooster drawings in the *Strega Nona* books

Function Goals

- Its wings must flap and its head must turn
- Operated from underneath so it will need to be a rod puppet
- Operated by a small child—the mechanism must be simple and strong

Tools

Scissors for foam and fabric
Glue gun

Materials

Urethane foam for body structure and under layer of wings
Polyfill for wings
Spray adhesive for urethane foam
Hollow tube (CPVC) to attach to inside of rooster's neck and serve as the rod to support the puppet
Rigid rod (dowel) to fit inside hollow tube and attach to the rooster's head; should be at least 8" longer than the hollow tube at the bottom for the head-turning mechanism
Stretchy fabric for covering
Steel boning to stiffen wings and serve as pull points for wing-flapping mechanism
Strong nonstretch cord for wing flapping
Ring for pull cord
Pigment in medium
Hot glue
Silamide

Structure Techniques

Sculpt shape with urethane foam:
- Pattern and cut body shapes out of foam
- Glue body together, leaving a temporary opening at head and back of neck, and a larger, permanent opening at bottom

Detail Techniques

- Apply stiffener:

    Assemble wings with adhesive (each wing is made of polyfill and one piece of foam) with a length of steel boning securely glued inside and extending to the outside at least 2" (to be trimmed later) at the point of attachment to the body

    Glue the outside of the top end of the CPVC to the inside of the neck of the rooster for strength

    Place the dowel inside the CPVC so that the top end of the dowel extends beyond the top of the CPVC into the inside of the head of the rooster. Glue very securely in place so that when you have one hand holding the CPVC and the other twisting the dowel, the rooster's neck will hold still and his head will turn

    Once you are satisfied that this mechanism will work and will be strong enough to last, glue rest of foam seam closed at the head and neck

- Rig moving parts:

    Cut slits in the foam body on each side where the wings should attach.

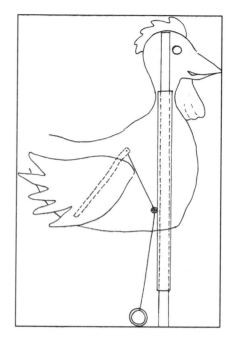

Bind them with gaffer's tape so they don't tear

Trim steel boning that sticks out of each wing to 1" or so beyond wing edge

Punch hole just in from end and attach a length of cord to each wing

Thread cords through reinforced slits, pull wings into the body of the rooster, and test wing flapping by pulling down on cords—wings should flap up without obstruction; trim, fix, and otherwise adjust until they do

Insert cords through slits again to put wings in place. This time sew the fabric of each wing to the fabric at each slit, to form a hinge and keep the wings attached to the body; add legs and feet

- Pad shape with polyfill: Cut, stitch, and stuff red rooster comb and glue to top of head. Repeat for wattle at throat

Surface Techniques

- Cover surface with fabric: Cut, stitch partly around, turn, fit and stitch by hand stretch terry cloth coverings for the body and two wings, taking care to add little pieces of the fabric either side of each slit to allow fabric to then be pulled to inside of foam body and stitched in place to finish edges of slits
- Soft sculpt details: If desired, machine stitch feather detail onto each wing, stitching through all layers of fabric and foam. Take care to avoid hitting steel boning
- Paint surface: Lay base coat of pigment in medium on all three pieces while they are separate

TALKING TIGER RUG

from *Me and My Girl*

This stage prop and its two mechanisms are just the beginning of all the visual surprises in the first scene of Act Two of the musical *Me and My Girl*. It has to look like a rug, act like a hand puppet, wiggle its ears, and then disappear! This is the piece that led me to discover that I could build animals—and we've since gone on to reach new heights of silliness.

Appearance Goals

Built for the musical *Me and My Girl* and must look like a real tiger that's been made into a rug

Function Goals

- Tiger must be able to "talk"—the actor sitting next to it must be able to manipulate its lower jaw inconspicuously
- Ears must wiggle on cue
- Entire piece must be light and indestructible enough to be whisked off the set every performance by its tail and not get damaged

Tools

Glue gun
Serrated knife
Surform
Orangewood stick

Materials

Ethafoam plank
Pile fabric
Dowels for the mouth mechanism

Hollow tubing, springs, cord, and ring for the ear wiggling
Friendly plastic for nose, eyes, teeth
Plastic animal eyes
Pigment in medium for nose and eyes
Leather for jaw hinge
Rabbit fur around eyes, inside ears, and at snout
Hot glue
Spray adhesive

Structure Techniques

- Sculpt head with ethafoam plank
- Make rug "body" with fabric

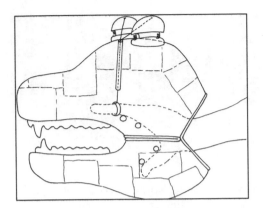

Detail Techniques

- Add facial details: Place eyes; sculpt teeth, nose, ears, and eye sockets with Friendly plastic
- Rig moving parts: Connect lower jaw with leather "hinges"; connect Friendly plastic eartops to head with springs; install wire loop at tip of each ear for cord; rig pull mechanism for ear wiggling; install dowels in upper and lower jaw for puppeteering

Surface Techniques

- Paint the surface: Paint nose, eye sockets, and gums with black pigment in medium
- Cover surface with fabric: Cover ears with fur on front and fabric on back; cover around eyes and nose with fur; cover inside of mouth with red fabric; cover outside of head with pile fabric; add heavy red base fabric to underside of body "skin"

Appearance Goals

The aging stripper costume has to have exaggerated, heavy, swinging breasts in a costume that is essentially the same style as those worn by the young chorus dancers. While the young chorines sing "take it all off," the aging chorine sings "put it back on."

Function Goals

Breasts have to "swing" by themselves when dancer moves slightly

Tools

Overlock sewing machine

Materials

Stretchy fabric "sacks"
Dried peas
Fringe, sequins, and tassels for trim
Silamide

Structure Techniques

Make garment shape with fabric: Use a four-thread overlock seam for strength

Detail Techniques

Pad shape: Fill with dried peas

Surface Techniques

Add found object details: Trim to match the young chorine costumes

This Red Death costume was a last minute add-on—you know the story, they were supposed to come from another rental house and weren't what the customer wanted. We weren't given much time to produce three of these costumes and hats, and had to find a way to replicate opulence quickly.

Appearance Goals

Stylized costume, built for the masked ball scene in a production of *The Phantom of the Opera*, that has oversized fronts and cuffs, which needed to have the look of heavy gold embroidery

Function Goals

- No time or money to actually embroider the garment
- Needs to be made of a washable fabric as drycleaning solvents will dissolve polymer medium (slipper satin will machine wash nicely on gentle cycle but do not let it spin too much; then hang and let air dry)

Tools

#8 round paintbrush

Materials

Costume pieces cut out
Bronzing powder and medium
Stencil

Structure Techniques

In this case, paint the surface decoration on before the garment is sewn together because the pieces are flat and smaller than the finished garment will be, making them easier to handle

Detail Techniques

None

Surface Techniques

Paint with bronzing powder and medium freehand to fill in spaces; when paint is dry, put costume together

WILL'S SISTER

from Will Rogers Follies

Appearance Goals

- A set of costumes for a production of *Will Rogers Follies*
- Designer wanted artificial sunflowers on them

Function Goals

Rental house wanted them to be machine washable

Tools

Glue gun
Needle
Silamide

Materials

Artificial flowers
Felt
Snaps
Hot glue

Structure Techniques

Shape with fabric: Make felt circles large enough to cover center of back of flower, but small enough not to show from the front; arrange flower petals in a pleasing way

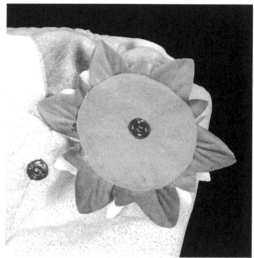

Detail Techniques

Apply connectors:
- Sew one side of a snap to one side of the felt

- Hot glue the back of each flower to the plain side of a felt circle
- Sew the other half of each snap onto the costume where the flower is

Surface Techniques

Add found object details: Snap the flowers onto the costume for a decorated look; remove them for washing the costume

Appearance Goals

Must look like heavy metal chain mail for a Shakespearean battle scene

Function Goals

Must be comfortable to wear and easy to clean

Tools

Knitting machine (or knitting needles)

Materials

Rug yarn
Bronzing powder and medium

Structure Techniques

Shape garment with yarn: Knit rectangles of the desired shape

Detail Techniques

Sculpt detail by assembling the pieces into garment parts. Most are tubes—sleeves, legs, hood. May be sewn onto a fabric base for strength

Surface Techniques

Paint/texture surface: With the purl side out, brush bronzing powder in medium over the loops of the purl stitches, which gives the illusion of heavy chain link

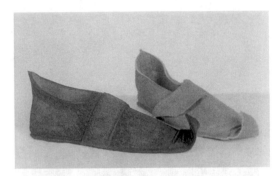

We made these shoes and the elf costume for a state lottery TV commercial a number of years ago. We never did get to see, meet, or fit the actor until the day of the shoot, and boy, was it a relief when everything fit and looked right! The actor was five-feet-ten-inches tall and was supposed to look like a four-foot-tall elf. To create that illusion, he sat on a giant mushroom and was surrounded by oversized props. He was supposed to be centuries old, having just come into the present day to promote the sponsor.

Appearance Goals

Must look well worn, like shoes that an elf has been wearing for years, tromping through the woods

Function Goals

Must be made new, using stylist's design, to fit non-elflike actor

Tools

Leather needles
Heavy-duty sewing machine
Paintbrush

Materials

Leather for uppers
Sole leather
Permanent marker
Leather shoe dye

Structure Techniques

Shape with leather: Sew pieces together

Detail Techniques

Apply connectors: Add hook-and-pad closure

Surface Techniques

Paint color/texture on the surface with desired color leather dye, then "age" with permanent marker

LATEX ARMOR

Appearance Goals

Built for the musical *Pippin*, must look like metal armor, but highly stylized

Function Goals

Must be flexible enough so the actor wearing it can dance

Tools

#8 round brush
Paintbrush

Materials

Casting latex
Gauze
Talc
Negative plaster mold
Bronzing powder in acrylic medium
Pigment to color the latex

Structure Techniques

Create structure with slush latex in negative mold:
• Add pigment to slush latex for desired color—black is good
• Place layers of gauze between layers of latex for strength, as follows:

Pour first layer, let set, then pour off excess

While still wet, press layer of gauze into wet surface, let dry enough to stabilize the gauze

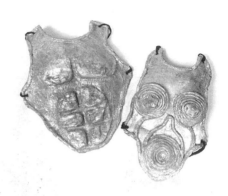

Repeat until piece is thick enough—about 3/8″
• Let surface dry completely, dust with talc
• Pull piece from mold

Detail Techniques

Apply connectors: Add grommets and ties

Surface Techniques

Paint color/texture on surface with bronzing powder in medium over surface of piece for metallic finish

SALIERI MASK

from *Amadeus*

Appearance Goals

Built for the musical *Amadeus*, this mask must look menacing, but still show the actor's lower face

Function Goals

- Must be strong as it will go into rental stock
- Worn by actor for most of the show, so it can't be too heavy

Tools

Scissors
Paintbrush
Pan with water
Clothespins

Materials

Ready-made half mask for shape of structure
Plaster bandage
Sculpt or Coat® and pigment for color and strength
Felt hat form
Black fabric for drape over hat form

Structure Techniques

Start with found shape: In this case we purchased a mask

Detail Techniques

Sculpt detail / add contours:
- Use plaster bandage over found shape
- Build up and refine contours where desired with pieces of paper toweling
- Drape again with plaster bandage

Surface Techniques

- Paint color / texture surface:

    Use black pigment in Sculpt or Coat®

    Highlight details with white pigment in Sculpt or Coat®

- Add found object details: Attach the top of the mask to a soft hat form so that the hat fits firmly on the actor's head and supports the mask in position. Conceal the hat form with a black drape that extends from the upper edge of the mask over the head to the neck, thus concealing the hat form and the actor's head, neck, and ears, making him very mysterious

CROWN

from Me and My Girl

Appearance Goals

Must look like the original style of an English peer of the realm in musical comedy fashion: gold balls on upright posts rise out of a band of ermine that surrounds the head, and red fabric fills the center to cover the hair

Function Goals

Must be lightweight and stay on while the actor moves energetically

Tools

Scissors
Zigzag sewing machine
Wire cutters
Pliers for bending wire
Glue gun

Materials

Stiff stuff headband joined with wide elastic at back
Millinery wire
Styrofoam balls
Coat-hanger wire to support balls
White pile fabric to simulate fur
Bronzing powder in medium
Hot glue

Structure Techniques

Shape garment with fabric: Cut a band of two layers of stiff stuff about three inches wide and about twenty-two inches long

Detail Techniques

Apply stiffener:
- Zigzag millinery wire all around long and short edges of band
- Stitch about two inches of wide white elastic to the short ends to join the band into a round shape
- Cut coat-hanger wire into eleven- or twelve-inch lengths; bend into U shapes so that there is a right angle bend four inches from each end of each piece

- Hand sew U-shaped pieces of coat-hanger wire around the inside, so that the open ends of the Us are evenly spaced to position the gold balls on top

Surface Techniques

- Paint color / texture on surface:

  Paint the surface of the balls with medium and gold bronzing powder

  Push one ball onto each wire post and carefully hot glue it into place

- Cover surface with fabric:

  Cut white pile fabric about twenty-six inches long and six inches wide

  Sew short ends together

  Fold in half lengthwise, place fold at bottom of band and pull up to cover both inside and outside of crown band, then handsew in place around uprights

  Add "tails" of black fur (we keep an old black fur coat sleeve just so we can cut fake ermine tails from it) or use a permanent black marker to create the same effect

MIDSUMMER CROWNS

from A Midsummer Night's Dream

Appearance Goals

Built for a semitraditional production of A Midsummer Night's Dream, the crowns for the King and Queen of the Fairies need to reflect the lightness and whimsy of fairies, but also the power these two rulers have

Function Goals

Built for rental stock, the crowns must be strong and sturdy while still looking ethereal and fragile

Tools

Wire cutters
Zigzag sewing machine
Glue gun

Materials

Stiff stuff
Millinery wire
Costume fabric
Stylized wig for each character
Hot glue

Structure Techniques

Shape garment with fabric:
- Cut the crown shapes of stiff stuff and covering fabric
- Stitch layers together around all edges

Detail Techniques

Apply stiffener: Zigzag milinery wire to all edges, then join ends to form circle

Surface Techniques

Add found object details: Hot glue sequin trim around top and bottom edges, then hand sew onto wig

EAGLE TRICORNE

from Cabaret

Appearance Goals

Built for the musical *Cabaret*, the designer specified a tricorne hat with an oversized American eagle mounted on the crown

Function Goals

Must be lightweight and able to balance on the head of a dancing chorus girl

Tools

Serrated knife
Surform
X-Acto knife for detail sculpting
Glue gun

Materials

Ready-made tricorne
Ethafoam plank for eagle
Coat-hanger wire for legs and mounting structure
Air-drying clay for feet
Royal blue lamé to cover hat
Gold bronzing powder and pigment in medium
Hot glue
Silamide
Gauze
White glue

Detail Techniques

- Apply connectors: Bend one end of short length of coat-hanger wire to form center of "foot," then insert other end of coat-hanger wire into each leg, and hot glue in place
- Sculpt detail: Sculpt feet with air-drying clay

Structure Techniques

Shape with ethafoam plank: Eagle is carved out of a single sheet of ethafoam

- Apply connectors:

    Bend the middle of another piece of coat-hanger wire into a circle and then bend that circle to a 90° angle to the ends

    Insert the ends into the back side of the eagle far enough so that when the circle is resting on the crown of the hat, the eagle is supported high enough for feet to clear it; hot glue it in place

    Test eagle on hat for size and balance, then hot glue eagle in place on mounting

Surface Techniques

- Cover surface with fabric: Cover hat with royal blue lamé
- Paint color/texture on surface: Coat eagle with bronzing powder in medium; paint features and details with pigment in medium
- Sew mounting with eagle on it in place on hat

EGYPTIAN HEADDRESS

Appearance Goals

Built for the musical *Joseph and the Amazing Technicolor Dreamcoat*, the headpiece should look like an Egyptian headdress but styled for a musical comedy—that is, fun, but not irreverent

Function Goals

Must be lightweight and easy to wear

Tools

Zigzag sewing machine

Materials

Headdress fabric
Stiff stuff
Elastic
Air-drying clay
Bronzing powder and medium

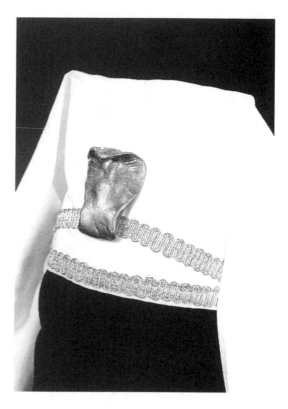

Structure Techniques

Shape garment with fabric: Cut and sew headdress with stiff stuff and elastic

Detail Techniques

Sculpt detail: Sculpt asp with air-drying clay to be proportionally pleasing

Surface Techniques

Paint color/texture surface: Coat asp with bronzing powder in medium, then sew it to the headdress

MIKADO HEADPIECE

from *The Mikado*

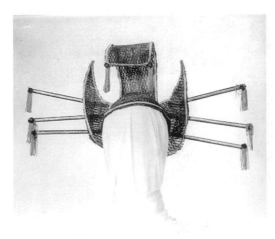

This headpiece was one of my first adventures with thermoplastic mesh, and I thoroughly enjoyed the speed and ease with which it went together. I also found out what the word *thermoplastic* really meant. I took the crown with me one summer to exhibit at a show and laid it on the front seat of my car while I went to have breakfast. When I came back out to the car, I found that my headpiece was as flat as a pancake, having sat in the sun for about forty-five minutes! It was still soft, and I took it out of the car and into the shade. I propped the hat part into a round shape with one hand while draping the top piece over my other forearm and, in that position, waved the piece back and forth in the air till it finally felt firm and went back into shape again.

Appearance Goals

Built for a production of the Gilbert and Sullivan operetta *The Mikado*, the headpiece had to be the traditional shape for a Japanese emperor

Function Goals

Needs to be lightweight and adjustable in size

Tools

Heavy-duty scissors
Hot water bath for thermoplastic
Glue gun
Paintbrush

Materials

Thermoplastic mesh
Steel boning
Hot glue
Pigment in medium
Bronzing powder in medium
Tassels

Structure Techniques

Shape with thermoplastic mesh

Detail Techniques

Apply stiffeners: Hot glue on spines

Surface Techniques

- Paint color/texture on surface: Use pigment in medium and decorate with bronzing powder in medium
- Add found object details: Hot glue on tassels

What a challenge! I've built warbonnets before, from a kit, and knew how they should go together, but working out exactly how to do it when the feathers are longer, heavier, and have to be suspended in a different place and in a somewhat different way was another thing entirely!

Appearance Goals

Built for a production of *Will Rogers Follies*, this headpiece needed to be constructed like a traditional Native American warbonnet, but with fancier materials for this Ziegfield-style musical spectacle

Function Goals

Even though the warbonnet is larger-than-life, it has to be sturdy enough for a fast backstage change *and* be stable on the chorus girl's head as she dances and walks up and down stage stairs

Tools

Glue gun
Pins

Materials

24″ ostrich feathers
Bamboo barbecue skewers, to support height of feathers
Felt bonnet
Gold lamé lacing
Marabou with Lurex

Mirrors
Short, fluffy feathers
Silamide

Structure Techniques

Start with found shape: Use felt hat base and trim to create traditional warbonnet shape

OSTRICH WARBONNET

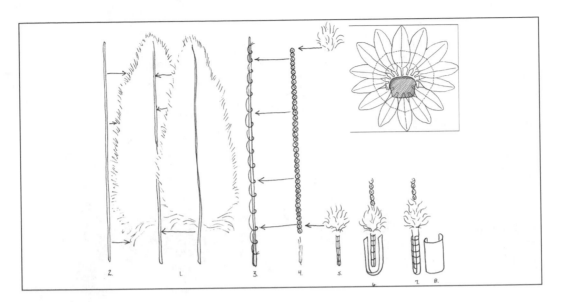

Detail Techniques

- Sculpt detail of each feather as follows:
  1. Hot glue spines of two ostrich feathers together
  2. Hot glue bamboo skewer onto back of rear spine for strength
  3. Sew spines of the two feathers and skewer together with slipknots
  4. Hot glue strip of sequins to front of spine for decoration
  5. Hot glue short fluffy feather to top and bottom of each ostrich feather
  6. Hot glue 1/4" metallic tape around bottom end of spines loosely enough to form loop
  7. Stitch and glue into place, leaving loop exposed
  8. Wrap ends of tape and bottom of spines with piece of lamé fabric about 2" x 1" and sew in place

- Apply connectors:

  Attach loops of feathers around edge of felt hat base

  Space feathers by attaching a piece of narrow ribbon to the back of each spine a little less than halfway up the length

  Start with center front feather and work the ribbon around so that the feathers begin to flare outward more as you get around each side and drape downward at the back, in the traditional warbonnet style

Surface Techniques

Add found object details: Decorate front edge of hat base with marabou; add strips of marabou boa to each side; cover top edge at temples with round mirrors

TAMBOURINE HAT

Appearance Goals

Built for a production of *Will Rogers Follies*, this hat needed to look like a straw boater from the Roaring Twenties

Function Goals

- We used Styrofoam boaters, because they were economical and are much easier to cut little windows in
- Need to install tambourine jingles in the crown for music

Tools

Knife

Materials

Ready-made Styrofoam boater
Tambourine jingles
Sculpt or Coat®

Structure Techniques

Start with found shape: Use ready-made Styrofoam boater

Detail Techniques

- Apply stiffener: Coat hat with 7 or 8 layers of Sculpt or Coat® for strength
- Sculpt detail: Cut rectangular windows in crown

Surface Techniques

- Add found object details: Install jingles and add ribbon around base of crown
- Paint color/texture on surface with final layer of Sculpt or Coat® to seal on details

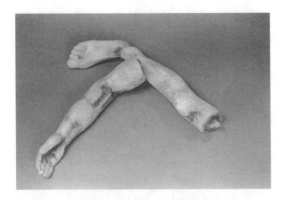

Appearance Goals

- Body parts created as props for the war segment of the quirky, medieval musical comedy *Pippin*
- Parts have to be strewn around the stage to depict the ravages of war, but should not be too gory

Function Goals

Cannot be fragile, as they get tossed around a bit onstage

Tools

Serrated knife
Surform
Gluegun

Materials

Ethafoam rod in three- and four-inch diameters
Hot glue
Pigment in medium

Structure Techniques

Shape with ethafoam rod

Detail Techniques

Sculpt detail:
- Cut wedges, bend, and hot glue at angles for elbows, knees, ankles
- Sculpt with knife and surform for fingers and toes

Surface Techniques

Paint color/texture on with pigment in medium

HARP

from *Into the Woods*

Appearance Goals

Constructed for the musical *Into the Woods*, this needed to be both a fairy-tale– and musical comedy–style harp

Function Goals

Must move on, off, and around the stage by pushing the top of it: the frame has to be strong, and the wheels have to work well

Tools

Jig- or band saw, to cut plywood
Hot glue gun, for ethafoam
Scissors
Paintbrush

Materials

Plywood frame and base
Wheels for base
Ethafoam rod, for shaping
Gauze, to wrap and strengthen integrity of piece
Bronzing powder and medium
Silly gold twisted paper for the strings
White glue
Hot glue

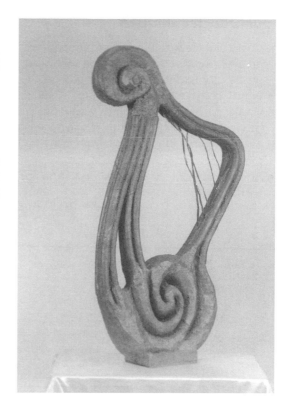

off so you won't be chasing your project all around the shop

Detail Techniques

Pad shape: Hot glue ethafoam rod around edge of harp for shaping both sides

Structure Techniques

Start with found (made) shape: Cut harp shape out of plywood and mount onto base; plan and set up method for attaching wheels to bottom of base, but leave them

Surface Techniques

- Cover surface with fabric: Coat remaining area of plywood and ethafoam rod with gauze dipped in diluted white glue
- Paint color/texture on surface: Paint whole piece black; dry brush with gold bronzing powder in medium, to give a lot of depth and illusion of weight to the piece
- Add found object details: Add strings with hot glue

Appearance Goals

- This is a walkabout costume that looks like the microphone of a two-way radio, which was used to promote a community safety program
- Needs to look friendly

Function Goals

- Needs to be able to get through doorways
- Does not speak or emit noise
- Wearer needs free use of hands to distribute literature about the program

Tools

Large scissors (or sharp knife)

Materials

Urethane foam for structure
Pile fabric for surface, so Radio Man looks accessible
Spray glue for both pieces of foam and fabric to foam
Stretchy fabric for viewscreen

Structure Techniques

Shape with urethane foam

Detail Techniques

Sculpt details: Cut eye and armholes; stitch wraparound glasses and apply to eye area (wearer will be able to see through the Lycra, even though others can't see in)

Surface Techniques

- Cover surface with fabric: Vellux gives a nice, smooth, but textured surface
- Add found object details: Apply letters with spray adhesive

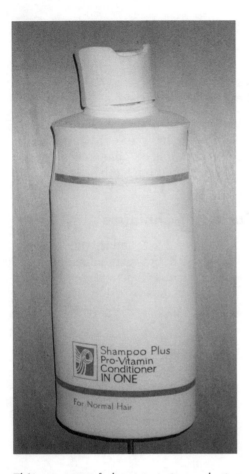

Appearance Goals

A walkabout costume that resembles a major brand bottle of shampoo for one-time use. The bottle cap was worn as a hat

Function Goals

Low-budget costume to be worn by a runway model; the costume doesn't have to do anything but look cute

Tools

Silamide
Scissors
Overlock sewing machine

Materials

Urethane foam for structure
Cotton Lycra for surface
Pigment in medium for decoration
Spray adhesive

Structure Techniques

Shape with urethane foam

Detail Techniques

Sculpt details: Cut out armholes

This was one of about twenty product costumes we built for an industrial show for the regional sales staff of a nationwide chain of discount stores. We were not given measurements, nor did we know who would wear which costume, so we simply assumed a set of standard model measurements. They all fit, and the show was a great success!

Surface Techniques

- Cover surface with fabric: Drape, pin, and stitch covering
- Paint color/texture on surface: Put cover on shape, draft graphics, remove cover, and paint. Taking the time to draft the graphics with the surface covering on the sculpted shape, then removing the surface covering from the shape and painting it flat actually saves time. Urethane foam is notoriously jiggly, and trying to paint straight-line graphics while the cover is on the foam takes more time and often results in a less than perfect job. Replace dry painted cover onto form
- Turn edges under and stitch

GHOST OF CHRISTMAS FUTURE

from *A Christmas Carol*

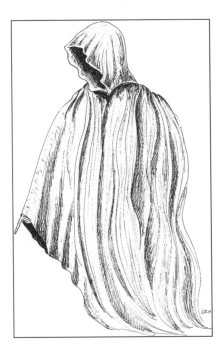

This was a remount of a previous production of A *Christmas Carol*, and the producers were happy with everything but the ghosts, which they wanted to be even larger-than-life. Since this ghost had to be twelve feet tall and hover just above the ground, it would have been easy to let this one get complicated, but I feel strongly that the simpler you can make a piece the more successful it will be. Elaborate mechanisms have a greater possibility of malfunction; add the tension of a production situation and you're asking for trouble.

Appearance Goals

- This spectre needs to be twelve feet tall and look as though it is floating just above the ground

- Except for the height and an eerie light inside the hood without a face, the look is the traditional black robe with deep hood and long skeletal finger pointing to Scrooge's grave

Function Goals

- Constructed as a giant rod puppet, it will have the mobility it needs
- Easily changed into and out of, as the actor plays other roles in this particular production
- The battery for the light source needs to be accessible so it can be replaced easily, even while the actor is wearing the puppet costume

Tools

Saws
Glue
Sewing machine

Materials

Backpack frame to raise shoulders
CPVC for extenders, arms, "bony finger," and lift poles for arms
Plastic bubble to fill hood
Small battery, lamp and switch, and lighting gel for color in the bubble (we used amber)
Quick links to hinge arms at shoulders, elbows, and wrist
Black cotton and tissue lamé for under and outer robes

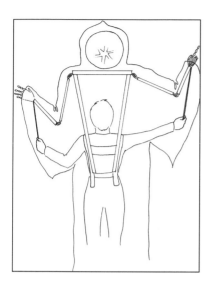

- Sculpt details: Cut out and bind off viewing rectangle in muslin underdress at actor's eye level (the actor will be able to see through the lamé, but not the cotton); rig bubble with small lamp colored with lighting gel (lamp dip)
- Apply connectors: Wire switch and battery at the actor's end of lift pole, then attach lift poles at wrists with quick links

Surface Techniques

Cover surface with fabric: Construct and attach hooded robe of black tissue lamé; be sure to include slits for lift poles for arms

Structure Techniques

- Start with found shape: Use backpack frame and CPVC extenders to raise top of frame; join extenders at top to form shoulders; link arm pieces to shoulders
- Shape garment: Construct the under robe of black cotton

Detail Techniques

- Apply stiffener: Attach plastic bubble at center of shoulder piece
- Pad shape: Attach very large shoulder pads to corners of upper structure for slight roundness

COWARDLY LION

from *The Wizard of Oz*

This is one example of a relatively simple hollow (not foam) latex mask-type prosthetic piece. Even though it was made for a particular person, and built on that person's life mask (see the life mask project), it will fit most adult faces pretty well. This one was done for *The Wizard of Oz*. It's also fun to do makeup on!

Appearance Goals

Partial (2/3) latex face mask of lion with cowardly expression

Function Goals

Needs to fit contours of an actor's face to enable him to sing

Tools

Orangewood stick

Materials

Life mask of the actor
Plasticine, a nondrying clay, to model features
Plaster, to make negative mold
Casting latex, to make mask
Pigment, to tint latex
Talc, for inside finished layer of latex

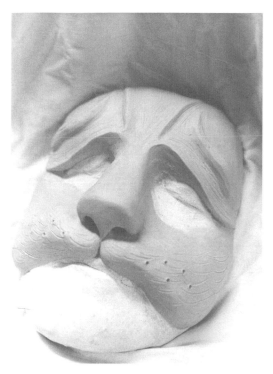

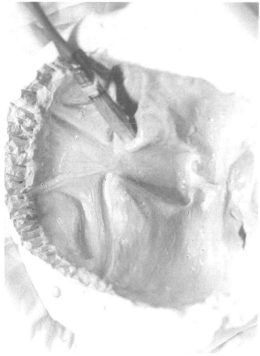

Structure Techniques

Create structure with casting latex in a negative mold:
- Sculpt lion features onto life cast of actor with plasticine, leaving the areas clear where the mask will be adhered to the actor so that the mask will be flush with the face (we added holes where we would later insert whiskers in the finished mask)
- Use a petroleum jelly release on the exposed areas of plaster cast
- Cast a negative plaster mold of sculpted face
- Clean up mold
- Paint desired number of layers of casting latex into mold
- Let each layer dry before adding another
- Dust inside of cured latex with talc

Detail Techniques

Sculpt details:
- Pull mask from mold and trim edges
- Wash off any small particles and let dry

PROSTHETICS

COWARDLY LION

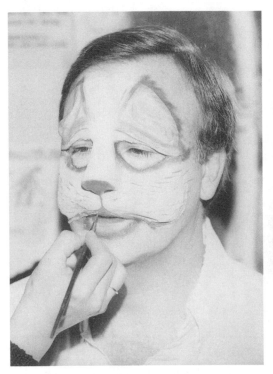 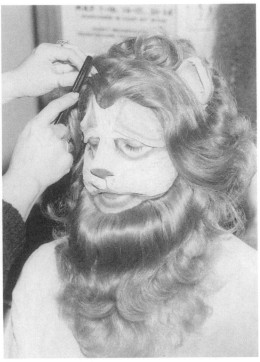

Surface Techniques

Paint color/texture on the surface: Apply mask to actor's face and then apply lion makeup to mask and face;

add beard and wig to complete

170

CHAPTER EIGHT

from Moby Dick

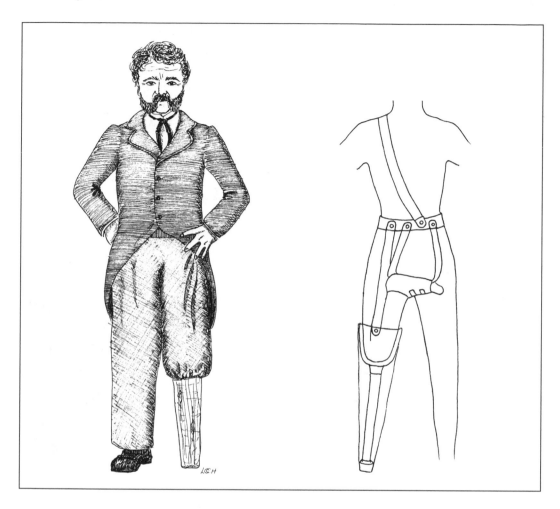

The appliance had to look like an ivory peg leg of the period for a production of *The Phantom of Life: A Melville Play*, by James Schiville, produced at the University of Rhode Island. When Joy Emery, the costume designer, called me to help with this prosthetic, I asked if an orthotist-prosthetist was being consulted. Joy assured me that was the first step she took; first and foremost the structure had to be safe for the actor to use. The project presented numerous challenges, and I felt privileged to be part of it.

Appearance Goals

The weight-bearing structure was created for us by orthotics-prosthetics specialists, who would also rig and fit the actor. The rigging included a cup, molded to the actor's bent knee, to which the two pegs would attach; the device that held and supported the actor's lower leg and foot was also developed by orthopedic specialists.

Our task was to create two cosmetic coverings for the artificial leg:

- An original peg leg with two removable "splinters" for the first encounter with the whale
- A second peg leg that was identical except that it was shorter and jagged at the bottom to look chewed off by the whale, for later in the play

Function Goals

- The actor has to stand, walk, and move about the ship on the peg leg; his own leg is bound behind his buttocks in an orthopedically safe way
- The actor has to still be able to do some weight bearing on the shorter stump

Tools

Heavy-duty scissors
Hair dryer
Sandpaper

Materials

Core of an artificial leg
Thermoplastic mesh
Air-drying clay
Pigment in medium
Velcro

Structure Techniques

Shape with thermoplastic mesh: Work both pieces at the same time so they are similar as needed

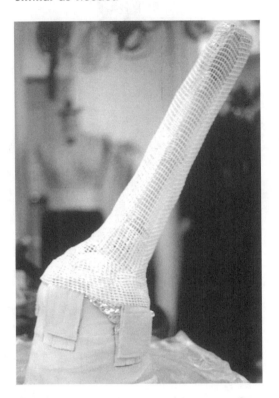

Detail Techniques

- Apply connectors: Sew and heat-bond hook-and-pad tape to the top end of each piece to correspond with the tape on the knee cup; these will hold peg leg coverings in place

- Sculpt details: Cut "splinters" from pieces of thermoplastic mesh; attach top end of splinter to the peg leg by tying to mesh frame. Bottom end of each splinter will attach with hook-and-pad tape after surface is created so it can be pulled away at the right time

  Coat shape with layers of air-drying clay to a smooth surface; dry each layer with a hair dryer before adding another; use sandpaper for final smoothness, if necessary
- Apply connectors: Attach pieces of hook-and-pad tape to bottom ends of splinters and point of attachment on peg leg

Surface Techniques

Paint color/texture on surface: Use pigment in medium to create ivory color and apply finish

A life mask is a plaster cast of a person's face. Creating one is a valuable process that every theatre student should undertake; both parties benefit because it is both personal and interactive. Unlike working with inanimate objects, the craftsperson must maintain a comfortable environment for the subject. This requires a lot of patience and sensitivity. Likewise, the subject must develop trust in the craftsperson, as he/she can only rely on nonverbal, nonfacial cues to communicate any discomfort.

Mastering this process and building a mask or other prosthetic from it teaches the basic techniques of all facial prosthetic work. An assistant is very helpful to have for this process.

NOTE: This process should be conducted in a quiet room, without disruption.

Appearance Goals

A base for creating other facial shapes, which can then be cast as prosthetics that will fit the face perfectly

Function Goals

- A great deal of care and preparation should be taken
- Not everyone is able to sit with his/her face completely covered in warm, wet heavy stuff with eyes and mouth closed for twenty minutes

Tools

Craft, or other type of, knife
Spoons
Bowls
Measuring cups

Materials

Pad and pencil for person whose face is being cast
Petroleum jelly to cover eyelashes, brows, and any other facial hair
Moulage (alginate)
Plaster bandage
Plaster

The Process

The steps of this technique are unique to this project. **Please note:** Follow all instructions in order. Those with an asterisk (*) may be assigned to your second pair of hands (if you are lucky enough to have one).

- *Begin to prepare the alginate

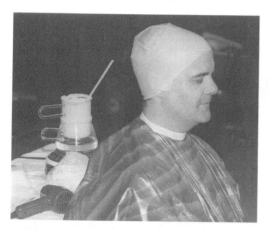

- Actor should sit up in a comfortable position, with head supported, feet on floor
- Talk through every step of the process before you begin
- The pad and pencil are for the actor to communicate if there is a problem (establish a hand signal as well—remember that *you* can speak to the actor, but *the actor* cannot see or speak to you)
- Inform the actor of each action you are going to do before and as you do them so the actor will know what is happening
- Coat all facial hair with petroleum jelly
- *Make sure that alginate is liquid and at a comfortable temperature before proceeding

- Begin placing softened alginate on actor's face—check with actor that temperature of alginate is okay—then work alginate into crevices at sides of nose, around lips, and over eyelids

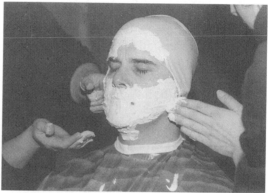

- Add more alginate to cover cheeks, forehead, chin, over eyes and around temples, continuously explaining in a soft and soothing manner to the actor what you're doing; bring the alginate near (but not over) nostrils (if you do this step carefully and slowly, you will not need to insert straws in the actor's nostrils)
- *Cut strips of plaster bandage and have bowl of water ready
- As soon as the alginate is built up to a minimum thickness of 1/2" all over the face, start draping softened strips of plaster bandage to strengthen the congealed alginate; using two layers, place the strips of the second layer perpendicular to the first and use smaller pieces around and between the nostrils
- *When the alginate begins to cool, mix the plaster according to directions, stirring very slowly to avoid creating air bubbles

- When the alginate is cool and the plaster bandage firm (you may want to use a hair dryer to move this part along), gently begin loosening the skin of the actor's face from the cast by pressing slowly and gently at the skin just outside the edges of the alginate and pulling outward toward the hairline, ears, and neck, working your way around the edge of the face
- Ask the actor to lean forward as you support the cast with one hand and the actor's back with the other to control the movement

- The cast should, with perhaps a little more help from you, release into your hand and leave the actor greatly relieved to have it over!
- *Help the actor to clean up, and listen to him/her talk about the experience; it will be helpful to the actor, and you can learn a lot about how to better do this next time!
- Fill the inside of the alginate cast with wet paper towels to keep it moist until the plaster is ready. Immediately begin placing small amounts of mixed plaster in each of the crevices of the alginate cast so you are sure every air space is filled

- Continue to fill the negative mold with plaster until it is full
- If you plan to hang this cast on the wall, you should now insert a small loop while the plaster is still wet

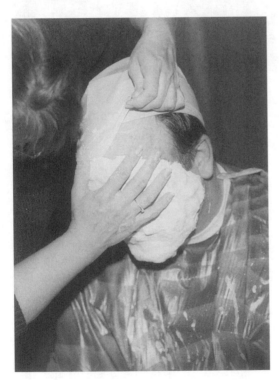

- Use a pointed object like a pencil to write identifying information in the semi-hardened plaster—the actor's name or initials and the date are appropriate, and add your own initials if you like
- You can smooth the surface with your finger, if necessary
- Carve out the nostril bumps so they look like indentations and fix any imperfections
- The plaster will become hot as it hardens and in about twenty minutes you can remove the alginate cast from the front of the plaster mold. Let the plaster cure for 24 hours before doing anything else to it

PROJECT	TOOLS	MATERIALS	STRUCTURE TECHNIQUES	DETAIL TECHNIQUES	SURFACE TECHNIQUES
Ass head	Cutting pliers Glue gun Clothespins	Round reed Fabric Found items Pigment in medium Urethane foam	Shape w/ round reed	Add facial details	Paint w/ pigment in medium Add found object details
Gypsy cow	Serrated knife Surform Glue gun	Ethafoam plank Pile fabric Balls—solid, hollow Hollow tubing Springs Weights Cord	Shape with ethafoam plank	Rig moving parts	Cover surface with fabric Paint eyes with pigment in medium Add found object details
Milky White cow	Surform Serrated knife Glue gun Pliers	Copper pipe CPVC pipe Ethafoam plank Nylon rope Springs Wheels Plaster bandage Pigment in medium	Assemble CPVC frame Shape with ethafoam plank	Rig moving parts	Coat surface with plaster bandage Paint surface of eyes with pigment Add found object details
Elephant skiing	Glue gun Sewing machine	Ethafoam plank CPVC pipe Felt Pile, other fabric Solid balls Flex screen Velcro Ethafoam rod Sequin trim Spray adhesive Steel boning	Shape with ethafoam plank Shape garment with fabric	Add facial details Apply connectors	Cover surface with fabric Paint color on eyes Add found object details
Hen	Zigzag sewing machine Cutting pliers	Ready-made hen Radio-controlled car Silamide Stiff stuff Millinery wire Stretchy fabric Pile fabric	Start with found shape	Apply stiffener	Cover surface with fabric
Lion, tiger skiing	Glue gun Serrated knife Surform Orangewood stick	Helmet liner Animal eyes Ethafoam plank Pile fabric Flex screen Friendly plastic Pigment in medium	Start with found shape Shape snout with ethafoam	Sculpt ears, eyes, jaw Sculpt teeth, nose Place flex screen	Cover with pile fabric Paint surface: nose, eye sockets

PROJECT	TOOLS	MATERIALS	STRUCTURE TECHNIQUES	DETAIL TECHNIQUES	SURFACE TECHNIQUES
Nana	Serrated knife Glue gun	Preformed head Ethafoam rod Pile fabric Flex screen Spray adhesive	Start with found shape Shape with ethafoam rod Shape body with fabric	Place flex screen	Cover with pile fabric
Rooster	Scissors Glue gun	Urethane foam Polyfill Spray adhesive Tubing Rigid rod Steel boning Cord Ring Pigment in medium Silamide Hot glue Stretchy fabric	Shape with urethane foam	Apply stiffener Rig moving parts Pad shape	Cover surface with fabric Soft sculpt details Paint surface
Tiger rug	Serrated knife Glue gun Surform Orangewood stick	Ethafoam plank Pile fabric Dowels Tubing Cord Springs Hot glue Ring Friendly plastic Leather hinges Animal eyes Pigment in medium Spray adhesive Rabbit or fake fur	Sculpt head with ethafoam Make rug body with fabric	Sculpt facial details Rig moving parts	Paint surface of features Cover surface with pile fabric
Aging stripper	Overlock machine	Fabric sacks Dried peas Fringe, sequins, tassels Silamide	Shape garment with fabric	Pad shape	Add found object details
Red Death	#8 round brush	Costume pieces Bronzing powder Medium Stencil			Paint color/texture on surface
Will's sister	Glue gun Needle Silamide	Artificial flowers Felt Snaps Hot glue	Shape with fabric	Apply connectors	Add found object details
Chain mail	Knitting needles or machine	Rug yarn Bronzing powder Medium	Shape garment with yarn	Sculpt detail	Paint color/texture on surface

PROJECT	TOOLS	MATERIALS	STRUCTURE TECHNIQUES	DETAIL TECHNIQUES	SURFACE TECHNIQUES
Elf shoes	Sewing machine Paintbrush Leather needles	Leather Shoe (leather) dye Permanent marker	Shape with leather	Apply connectors	Paint color/texture on surface
Latex armor	Paintbrush #8 round brush	Negative plaster mold Casting latex Gauze Talc Bronzing powder Medium Pigment	Create structure with casting latex in a negative mold	Apply connectors	Paint color/texture on surface
Salieri mask	Clothespins Scissors Paintbrush Pan with water	Half mask Plaster bandage Sculpt or Coat® Pigment Black fabric Felt hat form	Start with found shape	Sculpt detail	Paint color/texture on surface Add found object details
Me and My Girl crown	Scissors Zigzag sewing machine Pliers for bending Glue gun Wire cutters	Stiff stuff Styrofoam balls Coat-hanger wire Millinery wire Pile fabric Bronzing powder Medium Hot glue	Shape garment with fabric	Apply stiffener	Paint color/texture on surface Cover surface with fabric
Midsummer crowns	Wire cutters Zigzag sewing machine Glue gun	Hot glue Stiff stuff Costume fabric Millinery wire Stylized wigs	Shape garment with fabric	Apply stiffener	Add found object details
Eagle tricorne	Serrated knife Surform X-Acto knife Glue gun	Ready-made tricorne Coat-hanger wire Air-drying clay Fabric Bronzing powder Medium Silamide Gauze White glue Hot glue Ethafoam plank	Shape with ethafoam plank	Apply connectors Sculpt detail	Cover surface with fabric Paint color/texture on surface
Egyptian headpiece	Zigzag sewing machine	Headdress fabric Stiff stuff Elastic Air-drying clay Bronzing powder Medium	Shape garment with fabric	Sculpt details	Paint color/texture on surface

PROJECT	TOOLS	MATERIALS	STRUCTURE TECHNIQUES	DETAIL TECHNIQUES	SURFACE TECHNIQUES
Mikado headpiece	Heavy scissors Hot water bath Glue gun Paintbrush	Hot glue Thermoplastic mesh Tassels Bronzing powder Medium Pigment Steel boning	Shape with thermoplastic mesh	Apply stiffeners	Paint color/texture on surface Add found object details
Ostrich warbonnet	Glue gun Pins	24" ostrich feathers Short, fluffy feathers Felt hat form Gold lamé lacing Marabou with Lurex Silamide Bamboo skewers Mirrors	Start with found shape	Sculpt detail Apply connectors	Add found object details
Tambourine hat	Knife	Styrofoam boater Tambourine jingles Sculpt or Coat®	Start with found shape	Apply stiffener Sculpt detail	Add found object details Paint color/texture on surface
Body parts	Serrated knife Surform Glue gun	Ethafoam rod Pigment Medium Hot glue	Shape with ethafoam rod	Sculpt detail	Paint color/texture on surface
Harp	Jig- or band saw Glue gun Scissors Paintbrush	Plywood frame Wheels Ethafoam rod Gauze Bronzing powder Medium Twisted paper cord White glue Hot glue	Start with found shape	Pad shape	Cover surface with fabric Paint color/texture on surface Add found object details
Radio Man	Large scissors	Urethane foam Pile fabric Stretchy fabric Spray adhesive	Shape with urethane foam	Sculpt detail	Cover surface with fabric Add found object details
Shampoo bottle	Silamide Scissors Overlock machine	Urethane foam Stretchy fabric Pigment Medium Spray adhesive	Shape with urethane foam	Sculpt detail	Cover surface with fabric Paint color/texture on the surface

PROJECT	TOOLS	MATERIALS	STRUCTURE TECHNIQUES	DETAIL TECHNIQUES	SURFACE TECHNIQUES
Ghost of Christmas Future	Saws Glue Sewing machine	Backpack frame CPVC Plastic bubble CPVC adhesive Small lamp, battery, and switch Quick links Fabrics	Start with found shape Shape garment with fabric	Apply stiffener Pad shape Sculpt details Apply connectors	Cover the surface with fabric
Cowardly lion	Orangewood stick	Life mask Plasticine Plaster Casting latex Pigment Talc	Create structure with casting latex in a negative mold	Sculpt details	Paint color/texture on the surface
Pegleg	Heavy-duty scissors Hair dryer Sandpaper	Core of artificial leg Air-drying clay Pigment Medium Velcro Thermoplastic mesh	Shape with thermoplastic mesh	Apply connectors Sculpt details	Paint color/texture on surface
Life mask	Knife Spoons, bowls Measuring cups	Moulage Plaster bandage Plaster Petroleum jelly Pad and pencil	The steps in this technique are unique to this project		

COREY, IRENE. 1990. *The Face Is a Canvas: The Design and Technique of Theatrical Makeup*. New Orleans: Anchorage Press.

CORSON, RICHARD. 1989. *Stage Makeup*. Eighth edition. Englewood Cliffs, New Jersey: Prentice-Hall.

INGHAM, ROSEMARY, and LIZ COVEY. 1992. *The Costume Technician's Handbook*. Portsmouth, NH: Heinemann.

JANS, MARTIN. 1986. *The Art of Doing: Stage Makeup, Stage Makeup Techniques*. English edition distributed by Ruskin Book Services Ltd., Kidderminster, Worcestershire, UK.

ROSSOL, MONONA. 1991. *Stage Fright: A Guide to Health and Safety in the Theatre*. New York: Allworth Press.

ART CREDITS

The author and publisher wish to thank those who have generously given permission to reprint their work:

Photographs on pp. 30, 31, 33, 34, 41, 44, 45, 46, 48, 49, 62, 65, 69, 75, 79, 80, 81, 122, 123, 125, 130, 134, 136, 139, 142, 143, 145, 146, 147, 148, 149, 151, 153, 155, 156, 157, 159, 160, 161 by Phillip Austin of Austin Studio in Portsmouth, NH.

Photographs on pp. 168, 170, 174, 175, 176 by Karl Bye, Dover, NH.

Illustrations by Barbara Loch of Tracy Theatre Originals, Hampton, NH.

external hazard, 17
eyes, 27, 28, 29, 80, 101, 132, 139

F

fabric, 50, 52, 54, 87, 91, 111, 112, 122, 123, 129, 130, 132, 134, 136, 139, 141, 148, 149, 151. *See also* felt, gauze, lamé, Lycra, muslin, osnaburg, stiff stuff, stretch fabric, Vellux
feathers, 81, 157. *See also* marabou, ostrich, turkey
felt, 70, 75, 143, 148
fillings, 39. *See also* batting, pellets
flex screen, 51, 101, 103, 129, 132, 134
flowers, 82, 108, 118, 122, 143
foam. *See* urethane, ethafoam, rigid
found objects, 97, 111, 130, 134, 148, 151, 153, 157, 159, 166, 172
frame, 10, 73, 161
Friendly plastic, 107, 132, 139. *See also* thermoplastic
fringe, 118, 141
function goals, 2, 9
fur, 139

G

gauze, 54, 61, 112, 147, 153, 161
ghost, 1, 91, 102, 106, 108, 112, **166**
glue, hot, 27, 34, 41, 82, 122, 123, 126, 129, 132, 134, 136, 139, 143, 149, 151, 153, 156, 157, 160, 161, 166. *See also* hot melt glue
glue, white, 42, 112, 153, 161

H

hair, 77
hair dryer, 33, 172. *See also* heat gun
hands, 27, 28, 29
harp, 89, 102, 112, 116, 118, **161**
headpiece. *See* Egyptian, *Mikado*, warbonnet
heat gun, 27, 33. *See also* hair dryer
helmet liner, 132
hen, 97, 106, 112, **130**

hexcelite. *See* thermoplastic
holders, 27, 31
hook-and-pad tape, 48, 108, 129. *See also* Velcro
hot melt glue, 27, 34, 41, 89, 95, 104. *See also* glue
hydrocal, 63

I

Ingham, Rosemary, 91, 185
internal hazards, 15

J

jingles, 159
joiners, 27, 31. *See also* pins, tape, clothespins, adhesives, sewing machine, quick link

K

knitting machine, 145
knives, 27, 30, 68, 79, 89, 90, 96, 123, 126, 132, 134, 139, 153, 159, 160, 163, 174

L

lamé, 112, 113, 153, 166. *See also* fabric
latex, 61, 87, 93, 147, 168
leather, 12, 71, 75, 78, 104, 139, 146
life mask, 62, 63, 168, **174**
lion, 66, 89, 93, 97, 103, 107, 112, 114, **132**, **168**
Lycra, 52, 92, 102, 112, 164

M

magnets, 108
marabou, 157. *See also* feathers
mask, 62, 63, 64, 107, 116, 148, 168
materials, 2, 39
medium, 12, 53, 55, 88, 112, 114, 122, 126,

slush method, 93, 147
snaps, 108, 118, 143
spray glue, 163, 164. *See also* adhesive
springs, 45, 123, 126
stiffeners, 39, 51, 106. *See also* boning, felt,
    leather, stiff stuff, tubing, rod, wire
stiff stuff, 72, 106, 130, 149, 151, 155
stretch fabric, 112, 163. *See also* fabric
structure, 9
surform, 27, 33, 68, 79, 90, 123, 126, 132,
    139, 153, 160

T

talc, 94, 147, 168
tambourine hat, 106, **159**
tape, 27, 31, 89
tassels, 118, 141, 156
techniques, 2
texture, 52, 53, 56, 111, 112, 114
thermoplastics, 12, 65, 87, 95, 156, 172. *See
    also* Friendly plastic, hexcelite
thread, waxed, 46. *See also* Silamide
tiger, 1, 11, 66, 89, 91, 97, 101, 103, 104, 107,
    112, 114, **132, 139**
toluene, 21
tools, 2
trim, 39. *See also* balls, cord, ethafoam, eyes,
    feathers, flowers, wheels, fringe, sequins,
    tassels

tubing, 47, 73, 104, 123, 126, 139
turkey feather, 81. *See* feathers
twill tape, 44, 103

U

ultracal, 63
undercut, 112
urethane foam, 67, 87, 96, 122, 136, 163, 164

V

varaform. *See* thermoplastic
Velcro. *See* hook-and-pad tape
Vellux, 112, 163

W

warbonnet, 97, 116, 118, **157**
waxed thread, 46. *See also* Silamide
webbing, 44
weights, 123
wheels, 83, 126, 161
white glue. *See* glue, white
Will's sisters, 108, **143**
wire, 75, 149, 153. *See also* millinery wire
wood, 161